COMMUNICATING
EFFECTIVELY
WITH THE
CHINESE

Communicating Effectively in Multicultural Contexts

Series Editors: William B. Gudykunst and Stella Ting-Toomey

Department of Speech Communication
California State University, Fullerton

The books in this series are designed to help readers communicate effectively in various multicultural contexts. Authors of the volumes in the series translate relevant communication theories to provide readable and comprehensive descriptions of the various multicultural contexts. Each volume contains specific suggestions for how readers can communicate effectively with members of different cultures and/or ethnic groups in the specific contexts covered in the volume. The volumes should appeal to people interested in developing multicultural awareness or improving their communication skills, as well as anyone who works in a multicultural setting.

Volumes in this series

COMMUNICATING EFFECTIVELY WITH THE CHINESE

GE GAO

STELLA TING-TOOMEY

SAGE Publications
International Educational and Professional Publisher
Thousand Oaks   London   New Delhi

For information:

SAGE Publications, Inc.
2455 Teller Road
Thousand Oaks, California 91320
E-mail: order@sagepub.com

SAGE Publications Ltd.
6 Bonhill Street
London EC2A 4PU
United Kingdom

SAGE Publications India Pvt. Ltd.
M-32 Market
Greater Kailash I
New Delhi 110 048 India

Printed in the United States of America

Library of Congress Cataloging-in-Publication Data

Kao, Ko.
   Communicating effectively with the Chinese / by Ge Gao, Stella Ting-Toomey.
   p. cm. -- (Communicating effectively in multicultural contexts; vol. 5)
   Includes bibliographical references and index.
   ISBN 0-8039-7002-1 (cloth : acid-free paper)
   ISBN 0-8039-7003-X (pbk. : acid-free paper)
   1. Communication--China. 2. Intercultural communication--China.
3. Interpersonal communication--China. 4. Communication and culture--China. 5. Intercultural communication--North America. I. Ting-Toomey, Stella. II. Title. III. Series: Communicating effectively in multicultural contexts ; 5.
   P92.C5 K36 1997
   302.2'0951--ddc21
                                  98-19734

This book is printed on acid-free paper.
98 99 00 01 02 03 10 9 8 7 6 5 4 3 2 1

Acquiring Editor:	Margaret Seawell
Editorial Assistant:	Renée Piernot
Production Editor:	Sherrise M. Purdum
Production Assistant:	Karen Wiley
Typesetter/Designer:	Rose Tylak
Indexer:	Trish Wittenstein

Contents

Preface

"You speak very good English," a North American compliments a Chinese. The Chinese responds, "Oh, no! My English still needs improving." The North American is puzzled by the Chinese person's reply and the Chinese is unaware that he or she has violated an American cultural rule concerning how a compliment should be received. Intercultural communication styles and what constitutes appropriate and effective styles have always captivated our interest and fascination. This book is a reflection of that interest, and more important, it epitomizes our observation and experience of how Chinese communicate among themselves and with people from other cultures.

Chinese culture, along with other cultures, has its specific rules and norms for everyday social interaction. Variations in cultural assumptions, perceptions, and expectations often are grounds for intercultural miscommunication and misunderstanding. Questions such as what constitutes a polite interaction may provoke very different answers from people of different cultures. Consequently, both formal and informal exchanges in conversations among culturally different people can indeed be problematic. The goal of this book is to respond to this intellectual and pragmatic bewilderment, voiced by many people, by examining issues of communication in Chinese culture and in Chinese-Chinese and Chinese-North American encounters. It draws on work in communication, psychology, linguistics, and philosophy and utilizes the perspective of self and OTHER as a conceptual foundation for portraying and interpreting the dynamics of Chinese communication. Although this book is conceptually based, realistic instances of everyday talk will be incorporated to illustrate the specific characteristics and functions of Chinese communication.

A point of clarification is needed here for the terms *Chinese* and *North American*. *Chinese* refers to not only Chinese in mainland China, Hong Kong, and Taiwan but also those in Australia, Canada, Malaysia, Singapore, and the United States, as well as in many other geographical regions throughout the world. In this book, we do not suggest that Chinese are a homogeneous cultural group or that every Chinese person is a typical Chinese. Neither do we attempt to account for ways of communicating and relating of each and every aforementioned group. We hope, however, to provide an analysis of aspects of Chinese communication that, we believe, have transcended the geographical and political boundaries but, nevertheless, are distinctively Chinese. By the same token, the term *North American* does not imply every North American, given the ethnic and cultural diversity that exists in the United States. For the sake of the flow and readability of the book, we chose not to qualify terms such as *Chinese* and *North American* with *most*, *many*, *middle class*, *male*, or *urban* every time we used them. The generalizations we make refer to general patterns of communication with an understanding that individual and situational variations do exist.

This book is intended for anyone who seeks to have both a conceptual and a practical understanding of Chinese communication practices and their underlying cultural premises. After reading the book, the reader should have a good grasp of some prevalent cultural assumptions underlying everyday communicative activities in Chinese culture. Specifically, the reader should have a clear understanding how self-conception, role and hierarchy, relational dynamics, and face affect ways of conducting everyday talk in Chinese culture. Understanding the conceptual and practical issues discussed in this book will help the reader to better interact with Chinese. Those who share cultural characteristics with Chinese also may find our discussion of Chinese communication processes applicable.

The completion of this book would have been impossible without the contributions of many people. We owe an intellectual debt to those who have paved the way to a better understanding of Chinese people and whose work has been an integral part of this book. Among them, there are philosophers, psychologists, linguists, and communication scholars who deserve our special recognition. In addition, we thank Bill Gudykunst for his thoughtful support and encouragement. Bill has collaborated with us, at different times, on various studies concerning Chinese. His insightful suggestions and comments for this book are greatly appreciated. In completing this book, we have drawn extensively on materials from Gao (1996), and Gao, Ting-Toomey, and Gudykunst (1996). The writing of this book was also in part made possible by a faculty development grant from San Jose State University awarded to Gao. Last, but not least, we extend our special thanks to our loved ones—Trevor, Ian, Charles, and Adrian. Without their unending understanding and comfort, this book would not have been completed.

Ge Gao
Stella Ting-Toomey

1

Self-OTHER Perspective
and Communication

In today's world, national boundaries are constantly changing, and societies are moving toward greater interdependency and interconnectedness. The propensity of this increasing globalization poses unique challenges to the issue of how people from diverse cultural backgrounds attempt to effectively communicate on a daily basis. The need for effective communication in conjunction with cultural awareness, sensitivity, and understanding thus is intensified. As a result, the field of communication has been given an increasing amount of attention, and hence, the conception of this book is possible.

Chinese represent one of the largest cultural groups in the world and one of the prominent immigrant subcultures in the United States. There has been, however, little theorizing or research on communication in Chinese culture. To date, work of many Chinese scholars and others has centered on mass communication and international communication issues with little emphasis on face-to-face interpersonal interaction. An understanding and knowledge of ways of effective communication with Chinese is essential to the existence of global communities because it promotes appropriate and satisfying intercultural interactions.

1

Is communication an isolated event, or is communication connected with culture? In host-guest interactions, by rejecting a "no" as an answer to an offer of a drink, Chinese hosts show their hospitality. By accepting a "no" as an answer, North American hosts grant autonomy to their guests.[1] This difference illustrates that any communicative event does not take place independently; rather, it reflects how people in a culture perceive themselves and how they relate to others and their surrounding environment. In this chapter, we discuss the importance of adopting a cultural perspective in the study of communication. We begin by conceptualizing Chinese culture and communication. Next, we look at a conceptual framework in which Chinese communication is situated. We conclude by providing a preview of the following chapters.

◆ Conceptualizing Chinese Culture and Communication

The communicative behavior of Chinese intrigues many who have come into contact with it. To some, Chinese are shy, indirect, and reserved. To others, Chinese are evasive and deceptive. A single message can evoke entirely different meanings based on one's cultural upbringing and level of sensitivity to differences. In this section, we discuss the importance of cultural inquiry in the study of communication, examine how Chinese view communication, and delineate the functions of communication in the Chinese cultural context.

CULTURE AND COMMUNICATION

The notion of culture is vital to the study of communication because culture influences many facets of human communication. What message is sent, by whom, how, and in what situation, as well as what to say, when to say it, and how to say it, for example, are conditioned by culture. Culture helps define "appropriateness" of various communication behaviors, such as speaking, listening, silence, politeness, and turn-taking. People also draw on cultural knowledge to make conversational inference (i.e., to make sense of what is happening in a conversation), and conversational inference often is culture specific (Gumperz, 1994).

In essence, the culture in which a person is socialized and enculturated influences the way he or she engages in communication. Inevitably, the outcome of any communication is affected by how messages are presented and interpreted in a particular cultural context. To achieve effective communication in Chinese culture, therefore, requires a working understanding and knowledge of the Chinese social and cultural context in which communication takes place.

How then do we define culture, and how is Chinese culture similar to or different from other cultures? *Culture* can be defined in many different ways. In this book, we focus our attention on two ways of conceptualizing culture: (a) individualistic versus collectivistic value orientations and (b) low- and high-context communication styles. Both of these conceptions of culture have demonstrated their utility in explaining communication similarities and differences across cultures, and they serve as the basis for our subsequent discussions of Chinese communication processes.

Individualism and collectivism is one dimension of cultural variability utilized in the study of culture and communication (Hofstede, 1980; Triandis, 1988). Hofstede argues that people in individualistic cultures tend to emphasize self-actualization and individuals' initiatives and achievement, and they focus on an "I" identity. The United States is an example of an individualistic culture. Given the emphasis on an individual's rights, such as individuality, independence, and freedom, in the United States, family relations, loyalty, and harmony are perceived as less important (Chu, 1989). In collectivistic cultures, in contrast, people stress fitting in with and belonging to the in-group, and they focus on a "we" identity (Hofstede, 1980). Chinese culture is an example of a collectivistic culture. In addition, unique characteristics of collectivistic cultures are advanced by Triandis (1988). He argues that the in-group (e.g., family and work unit) is very important in collectivistic cultures. In a collectivistic culture, the needs, goals, and beliefs of the in-group often take precedence over those of the individual. Consequently, people in an individualistic culture exist as independent entities, whereas those in a collectivistic culture are defined by their in-groups. The individualistic aspects of the U.S. culture—such as focusing on an "I" identity, meeting one's own needs and desires, and being an independent entity—and the collectivistic aspects of Chinese culture—such as focusing on a "we" identity, meeting the needs and expectations of others, and being a part of the in-group—shape the distinctive communication processes present in those two cultures.

Another cultural dimension utilized in the study of culture and communication involves Hall's (1976) schema of low- and high-context communication. Hall argues that low-context communication emphasizes directness, explicitness, and verbal expressiveness, whereas high-context communication involves indirectness, implicitness, and nonverbal expressions. That is, "most of the information is either in the physical context or internalized in the person, while very little is in the coded, explicit, transmitted part of the message" (Hall, 1976, p. 79). Hall's descriptions of both the low- and high-context styles of communication provide a general characterization of U.S. and Chinese styles of communication, respectively.

It is important to point out that in this book, we refer to Chinese culture as a collectivistic and high-context culture and Chinese people as having collectivistic tendencies and using a high-context style of communication. We do not suggest that Chinese are a homogeneous cultural group or that every Chinese person is a typical Chinese. Neither do we attempt to account for ways of communicating and relating of each and every Chinese. As is well known, Chinese refers to not only Chinese in mainland China, Hong Kong, and Taiwan but also those in Australia, Canada, Malaysia, Singapore, and the United States, as well as in many other geographical regions throughout the world. We hope, however, to provide an analysis of some aspects of communication practices that, we believe, have transcended the geographical and political boundaries but, nevertheless, are distinctively Chinese. By the same token, even though we characterize North Americans as individualistic and as direct in their communication, we are aware of the cultural diversity that exists in the United States and fully recognize that not every person in the United States is a typical North American.

THE NOTION OF COMMUNICATION

The academic study of communication began after World War I in the United States (Littlejohn, 1992). The academic study of communication in Chinese culture, however, is a relatively recent phenomenon. Not surprisingly, most of the groundwork for research and theorizing in Chinese communication stems from work in Chinese philosophy, psychology, linguistics, and sociology.

Communication is a foreign concept to Chinese; no single word in Chinese serves as an adequate translation for the term. Many Chinese equate communication with talk. In Chinese culture, people who have the gift of talking, *neng shuo*[2] (能说), and are skillful in talking, *hui shuo* (会说), often are recognized as experts in communication. Communication, therefore, pertains only to a "privileged" few. This cultural orientation helps explain why communication has not been given a great deal of attention in the Chinese academic domain.

Although there is not a single Chinese term that corresponds to the word *communication*, there are several Chinese translations of the concept of communication. The three commonly used translations are *jiao liu* (交流; "to exchange"), *chuan bo* (传播; "to disseminate"), and *gou tong* (沟通; "to connect"). *Gou tong,* or the ability to connect among people, is the closest Chinese equivalent for communication as it is used by Western scholars. Yan (1987) argues that *gou tong* is the essence of human communication. *Gou tong* emphasizes the interactive nature of communication. In addition, *gou tong* articulates the nature, purpose, and characteristics of communication. The notion of *gou tong* is compatible with a view of communication as "the process by which we understand others and in turn endeavor to be understood by them. It is dynamic, constantly changing and shifting in response to the total situation" (Littlejohn, 1992, p. 7).

FUNCTIONS OF COMMUNICATION

Although the concept of communication may seem foreign to Chinese, they, like people in other cultures, engage in various communicative events—conversations, conflicts, debates, and arguments—in their everyday lives. In Chinese culture, not only is communication meaningful in its own right, but also, more important, it embodies both implicit and explicit assumptions, beliefs, and expectations. Specifically, we argue that the primary functions of communication in Chinese culture are to maintain existing relationships among individuals, to reinforce role and status differences, and to preserve harmony within the group.

For Chinese, maintaining relationships is an integral part of communication because the Chinese self is defined by relations with others, and the self would be incomplete if it were separated from others. The self can attain its completeness only through integration with others and its surroundings. Hsu (1971) indicates that Chinese make little distinction between themselves and others. The relational aspects of the self influence all facets of Chinese communication. Specifically, Chinese communication is not primarily utilized to affirm self-identity or to achieve individual goals but to preserve harmonious relations with family, others, and the surrounding environment. Verbal exchanges in Chinese culture, as Bond (1991) argues, are means of expressing affect and of strengthening relationship, whereas argumentative and confrontational modes of communication are avoided at all costs. Chinese communication, therefore, serves both affective and relational purposes.

Acting appropriately with appropriate people in appropriate situations not only determines the level of effectiveness in a communication transaction but also, more important, is essential to Chinese communication given that the Chinese self also is defined by hierarchy and role relationships. In a hierarchical structure, status is specified clearly, and behaviors are guided by the principle of *li* (礼 ; "ritual propriety"); that is, doing the proper things with the right people in the appropriate relationships (Bond &

Hwang, 1986). In Chinese culture, the sense of "self" is embedded within multiple prescribed roles. Cheng (1990) argues that it is the role, not the self, that determines the behavior. A state of *he* (和 ; "harmony") can be achieved if one maintains appropriate role relationships, is other oriented, and accepts the established hierarchy.

The ultimate goal of communication in Chinese culture is to preserve harmony. Harmony (*he*) is the foundation of Chinese culture. The Chinese term *he* denotes harmony, peace, unity, kindness, and amiableness. The principle of harmony permeates many facets of Chinese personal relationships. Chinese are inspired ideally to live in harmony with family members, to be on good terms with neighbors, to achieve unity with the surrounding environment, and to make peace with other nations. Seeking harmony thus becomes a primary task in the self's relational development and interpersonal communication. The appropriateness of any communication event thereby is influenced by the notion of harmony.

◆ Self-OTHER Perspective:
Contextualizing Chinese Communication

To make sense of Chinese ways of communicating, we must examine the underlying cultural assumptions, beliefs, and expectations concerning how Chinese perceive themselves and how they relate to others and their surroundings. In the previous section, we indicated that the notion of harmony, the relational self, and status or role are crucial to Chinese communication practices. In this section, we provide a conceptual framework that, we believe, serves as the foundation for our description, analysis, and interpretation of Chinese communication processes. We begin by presenting a Chinese concept of self. We then look at Chinese self in relation to Chinese family. Finally, we discuss the importance of hierarchy and role relationships in the development of self.

CHINESE SELF

The notion of self is important in explaining and interpreting many facets of human behavior. Self-conceptions influence how one relates to others in relationships and in everyday communication. In this section, we examine a Chinese concept of self and its implications in both personal relationships and communication in Chinese culture.

Conceptions of the Other-Oriented Self

In Chinese culture, self is formulated and expressed in a culturally specific way. Unlike the conception of an "individual" as an independent entity with free will, emotions, and personality, the Chinese equivalent of *individualism, ge ren zhu yi* (个人主义), implies selfishness and often is used in a negative sense (Hu & Grove, 1991). Sun (1991) argues that a Chinese "person" is not a complete entity. A person implies only a physical "body." An exchange of "hearts" (*xin*; 心) between two "bodies" completes a person (*ren*; 人). For example, a *ren* (人) is written with the character for "two" with a "human" radical (Sun, 1991).

The meaning of self has been explicated in different schools of thought in Chinese culture. From the Buddhist standpoint, there are two distinctive layers of self: the little self (*xiao wo*; 小我) and the great self (*da wo*; 大我). Although the little self seems comparable to the individual self, the great self is the true self devoid of individuality (Wu, 1984). Taoism defines self as part of nature. Self and nature together complete a harmonious relationship. Confucianism introduced both ethical and social implications to the Buddhist notion of self and suggests that the little self must succumb to the vision of the great self (Wu, 1984). Although Buddhism, Taoism, and Confucianism tend to differ in many fundamental ways, they all concur that self is not an independent entity and self is not complete by itself.

How then do we conceptualize a Chinese self? Confucianism asserts that individuality and the true self do not belong together;

rather, social and ethical responsibilities define the true self. This perspective has been a dominating force in casting the perceptions of the Chinese self and thus sets the foundation for our current analysis. On the basis of Confucianism, self is relational in Chinese culture. That is, the self is defined by the surrounding relations. Traditionally, the Chinese self involves multiple layers of relationships with others. A person in this relational network tends to be sensitive to his or her position as above, below, or equal to others (Chu, 1985; Fairbank, 1991; King & Bond, 1985). The relations often are derived from kinship networks and supported by such cultural values as filial piety (i.e., obedience to parents and financial support of parents), loyalty, dignity, and integrity. A male Chinese, for example, would view himself as a son, a brother, a husband, and a father but hardly as himself (Chu, 1985). Confucianism advocates that the "civilized" person should always be a responsible self, aware of his or her position in society and the world, and perform his or her duty accordingly (Chiu, 1984). In Chinese culture, to be aware of one's relations with others thus is an integral part of *zuo ren* (做人; "conducting oneself")—a Chinese person's lifetime goal. In essence, Chinese can never separate themselves from obligations to others (King & Bond, 1985), and Chinese self-esteem is connected closely with that of the collective.

The relational nature of the Chinese self is also a prevalent theme in both Chinese expressions and writings. *Da he you shui xiao he man, da he wu shui xiao he gan* (大河有水小河满, 大河无水小河干 ; "the tributaries are filled with water when there is water in the main stream and they dry up when there is no water in the main stream") and *chun wang chi han* (唇亡齿寒; "when the lips are gone, the teeth will be cold") demonstrate the interdependent relationship between the self and the collective. The late contemporary Chinese philosopher Hu Shi (胡适) (as cited in King & Bond, 1985, p. 31) asserted that, "In the Confucian human-centered philosophy, man [or woman] cannot exist alone; all actions must be in a form of interaction between man [woman] and man [woman]." This position is further articulated by Zhuang Zi (庄子) (329?-286 BC), who was believed to have written *Dao De Jing* (道德经) with Lao Zi (老子). Zhuang Zi wrote, "When you look at yourself as part of the natural scheme of things, you are equal to the most minute insignificant creature in the world, but your existence is great because you are in *unity* [italics added] with the whole universe" (as cited in Dien, 1983, p. 282).

The conception of the Chinese self coincides with the discussion of the interdependent construal of self (Markus & Kitayama, 1991). Markus and Kitayama contend that an interdependent self as opposed to an independent self is defined by relations with others in specific contexts. The components of *relation* and *other* are key to an interdependent self. Compatible with the interdependent construal of the self, the Chinese self also needs to be recognized, defined, and completed by others. *Bu fu hou wang* (不负厚望; "to live up to others' expectations") is aspired to and cherished in Chinese culture. Moreover, the Chinese self-development is connected closely with the self's orientation to others' needs, wishes, and expectations. In essence, the notion of other makes up an indispensable part of the Chinese self and thus permeates all indigenous concepts of Chinese interpersonal relationships and communication.

Implications for Chinese Behavior

The foregoing conceptions of the Chinese self help to shape Chinese communication assumptions and Chinese interpersonal transactions. Consequently, Chinese communication is situated in relationships rather than in individual persons, and others' interpretations and perceptions often define the meaning of an event. Yang (1981) points out that the importance of others in defining the Chinese self

> represents a tendency for a person to act in accordance with external expectations or social norms, rather than with internal wishes or personal integrity, so that he [or she] would be able to protect his [or her] social self and function as an integral part of the social network. (p. 161)

Chinese are brought up to *gu quan da ju* (顾全大局; "take the interests of the whole into account") rather than to be *he li ji qun* (鹤立鸡群; "like a crane standing among chickens") or *chu tou lu mian* (出头露面; "be in the limelight"). Yang (1981) further elaborates on the specific consequences of this other orientation as

> the Chinese's submission to social expectations, social conformity, worry about external opinions, and nonoffensive strategy in an attempt to achieve one or more of the purposes of reward attainment, harmony maintenance, impression management, face protection, social acceptance, and avoidances of punishment, embarrassment, conflict, rejection, ridicule, and retaliation in a social situation. (p. 161)

Research findings and observations appear to be congruent with Yang's (1981) assertions. The most persuasive argument for the reconciliation of broken marriages, for example, appeals to the needs and wishes of others, including children, family, and friends. In a well-publicized divorce trial in Shanghai in 1979, one broken marriage was reconciled for the sake of the child, the family, and the state. The judge even criticized the woman who initiated the divorce for lack of self-control (Dien, 1983). In community mediation, the feelings of others, harmony in the families and community, family reputation, and the respect of the neighbors are presented as important considerations to the disputants (Wall & Blum, 1991). Chinese often are concerned with what others will say, and this concern has a controlling effect on Chinese behavior.

In addition, observers of Chinese culture tend to describe Chinese as constantly referring to others' opinions and views and as unwilling to commit themselves to an opinion (Young, 1994). Cultural norms, such as modesty and humility (Bond, Leung, & Wan, 1982; White & Chan, 1983), reserve and formality, restraint and inhibition of strong feelings (Sue & Sue, 1973), as well as the use of shame and guilt to control behavior (DeVos & Abbot, 1966), all serve to reinforce the importance of others in one's relationships. To be modest is to treat oneself strictly and others leniently. Values such as tolerance of others (*rong ren*; 容忍), harmony with others (*sui he*; 随和), and solidarity with others (*tuan jie*; 团结)

(Chinese Culture Connection, 1987) further demonstrate this indispensable element of other in the conception of the self.

The emphasis on the relational and interdependent aspect of the self also has an impact on the Chinese self-concept. Chinese American graduate students and professionals, for example, report themselves as less active, flexible, attractive, sharp, and beautiful than European American graduate students and professionals (White & Chan, 1983). Following a person's success, Chinese college students in Hong Kong like humble or self-effacing attributions better than self-enhancing ones (Bond et al., 1982). Chinese are less likely than their North American counterparts to display pride in their success (Stipek, Weiner, & Li, 1989).

Relations not only define the Chinese self but also are an integral part of a Chinese person's life. Consider the following remarks by a Chinese sociologist: "In the unit system, keep[ing] good 'relations' becomes much more important than doing one's work well. Only the relations, not the work, count when it comes to promotions and welfare" (Link, 1992, p. 64). In Chinese grammar, interpersonal bonds are promoted and individual prominence is discouraged (Young, 1994). In extended Chinese discourse, for example, pronouns such as *I* or *you* and *we* or *they* can be discarded by interlocutors when referents are understood. A Chinese agent hence is embedded in a complex network of relationships. Conversely, the English discourse requires explicit subjects (Young, 1994). Young indicates that the "situation" focus in Chinese discourse and the "agent" focus in English discourse reflect views of self-conceptions deeply rooted in those two cultures.

FAMILY AND INSIDERS VERSUS OUTSIDERS

To gain a deeper understanding of the Chinese self, it is also important for us to examine the context of family. In Chinese culture, the family orients the self to others in terms of role obligations, status differences, in-group/out-group distinctions, and so on. Family thus provides an important context for the development of the Chinese self. Without understanding the impact of family and how the self relates to family members, insiders, and outsiders, it is impossible to fully explain and analyze Chinese communication practices and interpersonal relationships. We begin by looking at the notion of family. We conclude this section by examining the distinction between insiders and outsiders.

Family

Jia (家; "family") is the center of everything in Chinese culture (Smith, 1991; Tseng & Wu, 1985; Whyte, 1991). Although the structure of the traditional extended family has continued to decline in Hong Kong, Taiwan, and many places in China, the importance of family in many aspects of a person's life still prevails. To Chinese, a warm and close family remains the most important goal in life (Chu & Ju, 1993).[3] *Gu rou zhi qing* (骨肉之情; "feelings of kinship") rise above all other feelings. As the prototype of Chinese social organizations, family has significance to the study of family relationships in particular and interpersonal relationships in general. The rules and norms that guide family relationships apply beyond the boundaries of family.

Chinese perceive family as the foundation of society (Whyte, 1991). The following passage from the *Great Learning* (as cited in Whyte, 1991), one of the "Four Books" of Confucian learning, eloquently articulates the impact of family on Chinese society:

> By inquiring into all things, understanding is made complete; with complete understanding, thought is made sincere; when thought is sincere, the mind is as it should be; when the mind is as it should be, the individual is morally cultivated; when the individual is morally cultivated, the *family* [italics added] is well regulated; when the family is well regulated, the state is properly governed; and when the state is properly governed, the world is at peace. (p. 297)

In Chinese culture, a close relational bond exists between the self and the family. For the Chinese self, family serves as the primary and ongoing unit of socialization. Family is both a home and a community. In the family, one learns to communicate and relate to others, to give or receive support and comfort, to express oneself, and to acquire a relational identity. A recent study in China has shown that family members frequently interact with one another, and chitchat is the second most popular family activity (Chu & Ju, 1993). Thus, verbal expressiveness is a common practice among family members. In addition, parents often are sought for advice when children encounter problems (Chu & Ju, 1993).

Moreover, when friends become very close, Chinese consider them as members of the family (*peng you ru jia ren*; 朋友如家人). Consequently, kinship forms of address such as *uncles*, *aunts*, *sisters*, and *brothers* are adopted in social relationships. The term of address dictates a communication style that is appropriate in a given relational context. As a result, family practices come to be guiding principles in a larger social setting and help define what is appropriate and inappropriate behavior. Obligations to the family are also made known to the Chinese self. Research shows that Chinese children are taught to remember themselves as members of the family and to remember that what they do, good or bad, will affect the family (Chiu, 1984). The socialization process of the other-oriented self thus originates in the family.

The affinity and interdependence between the Chinese self and family present several limitations. Cheng (1990) points out that the Confucian "five cardinal relationships" (*wu lun*; 五伦) put too much emphasis on family and one-to-one relationships (e.g., brother and brother and father and son); hence, they fail to address the broader aspect of human relationship, such as that between a person and the community at large. Liang Qi Chao 梁启超 (1936), a prominent thinker in modern Chinese history, attributed a Chinese person's lack of "civic morality" (*gong de*; 公德) and sense of obligation to society to the Confucian ethic. Many instances in Chinese culture support this argument. Chinese are most likely to put family and one-to-one relationships before group or society. Family-centered rather than company-centered relationships constitute Chinese in-groups, and the in-groups are strong and stable.

Chinese charity patterns, for example, tend to center on kinship lines rather than on the general public. Stories are told about wealthy relatives helping extended families residing all over the world but giving little if any support to the local community.

Zi Ji Ren (自己人; "Insider") Versus Wai Ren (外人; "Outsider")

Scollon and Scollon (1991) noted, "Discriminating a boundary is not only a logical or a descriptive activity, it is a regulative and moral activity [in Chinese culture]. What is outside a boundary is not relevant in any way to what is inside" (p. 471). As Scollon and Scollon argue, the distinction between inside and outside influences interpretations in every aspect of Chinese culture. One such aspect deals with personal relationships in Chinese culture. Chinese make clear distinctions between insiders and outsiders. It is, however, in the Chinese family in which those distinctions are created and reinforced. The distinction between an insider and an outsider exists on all levels of interpersonal interactions. Y. J. Gu (1990) indicates that insiders consist of people from two categories: automatic and selected. Automatic insiders include one's parents, siblings, relatives, colleagues, and classmates. Selected insiders are special relations that one has developed over time at work or elsewhere. For example, one considers someone an insider at work after a special relationship has been developed through helping and sharing information with one another. The five common criteria of an insider are niceness, trustworthiness, caring, helpfulness, and empathy (Y. J. Gu, 1990).

The distinction between an insider and an outsider provides specific rules of interaction in Chinese communication and interpersonal relationships. Chinese tend to engage in honest and truthful conversations with insiders but are reluctant to disclose personal information to outsiders. This is indicative of the verbal expressiveness versus verbal restraint pattern present in the in-group versus out-group context. In personal relationships, Chinese focus on family, friends, and established relationships. There is, however, a growing tendency for Chinese to develop relational ties outside the kinship network, especially among those urban dwellers who are better educated and heavily influenced by the Western culture. Nevertheless, those relational ties are considered to be unstable and not as close compared with family relations or extended family relations (Chu & Ju, 1993). Moreover, Chinese may go beyond their means to help an insider, but an outsider has to follow the rules. A person with an insider status often enjoys privileges and special treatment beyond an outsider's comprehension. The insider-outsider distinction also involves moral implications. In Chinese culture, moral judgments are not only cognitively but also affectively based. Hwang (1990) indicates that moral standards tend to vary from one relationship to another. In essence, insiders often are treated differently from outsiders (Y. J. Gu, 1990).

The family-centered insider relationships bring forth two important implications for relationship development with strangers (i.e., outsiders). First, as King and Bond (1985) point out, the importance of family and the sense of dependency built up in the Chinese family system make it difficult to develop personal relationships with strangers. In general, Chinese are less likely to initiate interactions with strangers or to be involved in social relationships. In a recent survey, a vast majority of the Chinese respondents (84.5%) indicated that they would not trust a stranger until they became better acquainted with the person (Chu & Ju, 1993). The level of distrust placed on a stranger in a culture in which most relationships are based on preexisting conditions (i.e., a relative, a coworker, or a fellow classmate) is not surprising. In comparison with North Americans, Hong Kong students, for example, report fewer social interactions but more in-group interactions (Wheeler, Reis, & Bond, 1989). In Chinese culture, the transformation from a *wai ren* to a *zi ji ren* is an arduous and time-consuming process because personal relationships often take a long time to develop. After relationships have been developed, however, they tend to be very solid. Thus, to overcome this inherent difficulty in relationship development, intermediaries are widely used for social relational construction (King & Bond, 1985).

The second implication involves how value standards are applied to in-group and out-group members. Chinese and other collectivistic cultures tend to be particularistic in their utilization of value standards toward in-groups and out-groups (Hofstede, 1980; Triandis, 1988). That is, members of in-groups and out-groups are granted different value standards. The particularistic principle of interpersonal relationships hinders interactions with outsiders because value standards applied to in-groups may not be readily adapted to out-groups. Most Chinese do not feel competent or comfortable dealing with outsiders.

HIERARCHY AND ROLE RELATIONSHIPS

The conceptions of the Chinese self are also situated in, explained by, and governed by complex hierarchy and role relationships. In Chinese culture, the position one occupies and the role one plays define not only how one should perceive oneself in relation to others but also how one should engage in communication with others. In essence, the notions of hierarchy and role relationships permeate every aspect of Chinese society (Bond & Hwang, 1986; Taylor, 1989). They are central to our investigation of Chinese interpersonal relationships and communication because they form an underlying structure of what constitutes appropriate Chinese behavior in a given context.

In the Chinese hierarchical system, each person is presumed to perform his or her action in accordance to specific role functions. On the basis of the Confucian paradigm, the most important relationships in Chinese culture involve the five cardinal relationships (*wu lun*; 五伦), which are ordered by the rule of hierarchy. The five cardinal relationships are those between ruler and subject, father and son, husband and wife, elder brother and younger brother, and between friends (Cheng, 1990). The appropriate role behaviors associated with a person at the lower rank, such as subject, son, and wife, are those of obedience, respect, and submission (MacCormack, 1991).

The moral or social order in any culture, as Confucian belief proclaims, is maintained through the fundamental social roles played by parent and child as well as those by husband and wife (MacCormack, 1991). In Chinese culture, even the most intimate relationships, such as the relationship between husband and wife, convey a role-directed dimension. Ordering relationships by status and observing such order (*zun bei you xu*; 尊卑有序), for example, is considered a very important Chinese value (Chinese Culture Connection, 1987). Cheng (1990) argues that the role, not the self, determines the behavior in most East Asian cultures. Personal choices, therefore, are based on prescribed roles.

Chinese personal identities are connected closely with the social roles they play. The Chinese social code is of "acting a human being" (*zuo ren*; 做人) instead of "being" one (Sun, 1991, p. 20). A recent study shows that Chinese report paying greater attention to social comparison information (e.g., my behavior often depends on how I feel others wish me to behave) and others' status characteristics (e.g., I pay attention to my behavior when I am with someone older than I am) than do the English. The English, in contrast, report greater ability to modify their self-presentations, tendency to avoid public performances, sensitivity to others' expressive behavior, and self-monitoring than do Chinese (Gudykunst, Gao, & Franklyn-Stokes, 1996).

In Chinese culture, speech modification is necessary when one attends to rank, status, and hierarchy. Young (1994) observes that a "deferential" style of communication often is in order in the presence of authority. To be deferential, one needs to exercise both restraint and hesitance (Young, 1994). One should not, for example, present "definitive" statements in front of one's superior. The modified speech serves to reinforce status differences and create distance between superiors and subordinates.

The impact of hierarchy and role relationships on the Chinese psyche is best summarized by a young Chinese historian (Link, 1992):

> The habit of submitting to the group, or the leader, is too deep within us. A few days ago we had a seminar in our institute, where we talked excitedly about democracy and individuality for a whole morning.

The institute agreed to pay for our lunch that day, and our leader said, "Let's be democratic; let's have a vote about where to have lunch." No one could say anything. Everyone just looked at the leader. There were no suggestions. Finally the leader mentioned a few restaurants we could choose from and asked for opinions. Then a few opinions came out, but I still don't think they were individual preferences. They were just guesses at what people thought the leader wanted. (p. 133)

◆ Conclusion

In this chapter, we introduced the Chinese notion of communication and explained that the study of Chinese culture is essential to our understanding of Chinese communication processes. We then presented a conceptual framework on the construal of the Chinese self, suggesting that the Chinese conceptions of self are relational, other oriented, and influenced by complex hierarchy and role relationships.

◆ Organization of the Book

In this book, we intend to focus not only on specific communication behaviors that characterize Chinese but also on the larger cultural context in which Chinese communication is situated, understood, and analyzed. We intend to demonstrate that Chinese communication is not an isolated event but an integral part of all cultural phenomena. Therefore, the subsequent chapters in this book are designed to accomplish these objectives. In Chapter 2, our focus is on Chinese personal relationship development processes. Specifically, *gan qing* ("feeling"), *ren qing* ("human feeling"), and *bao* ("reciprocity") are discussed as representing core dimensions of affective experiences in Chinese personal relationships. The relational principles of *gan qing, ren qing,* and *bao,* as well as their implications for affective communication, are examined closely. In Chapter 3, we provide four enduring characteristics of Chinese communication: (a) *han xu* or implicit communication, (b) *ting hua* or listening centeredness, (c) *ke qi* or politeness, and (d) *zi ji ren* or a focus on insiders. We explore not only how these characteristics are conceptualized from the perspective of Chinese (i.e., an insider's view) but also their applications to understanding Chinese communication. Chapter 4 presents a brief review of different conceptions of *mian zi* ("face") and examines the impact of the concern for *mian zi* on Chinese communication and other aspects of a Chinese person's life. In Chapter 5, we identify and analyze the following eight areas of Chinese-North American miscommunication: (a) the importance of what is not said versus what is said, (b) the use of *we* versus *I*, (c) polite versus impolite talk, (d) indirect versus direct talk, (e) hesitant versus assertive speech, (f) self-effacing versus self-enhancing talk, (g) private versus public personal questions, and (h) reticent versus expressive speech. The chapter ends with a set of practical recommendations with regard to how Chinese can communicate effectively with North Americans and how North Americans can communicate effectively with Chinese. Throughout this book, by using specific interaction examples to illustrate different Chinese concepts, we aim to demonstrate that the self-OTHER perspective permeates all Chinese communication patterns. Understanding the relationship between the self-OTHER perspective and predominant Chinese communication styles will help reduce misattribution and misunderstanding between Chinese and others. Finally, issues and directions for future research in Chinese culture and communication are discussed in the epilogue.

Notes

1. In this book, our examples and analyses reduce communication to a dyadic interaction for the sake of demonstration. By no means do we suggest that communication is limited to two parties of interaction.

2. The indigenous Chinese concepts and names in this chapter are transliterated using the pin-yin system of romanization. For example, *bao* under the pin-yin system is equivalent to *pao* under the Wade-Giles system.

3. Successful children, career accomplishments, and a comfortable life are the other highly ranked important goals in life based on a survey of 2,000 respondents in Shanghai and its surrounding areas in China (Chu & Ju, 1993). Other results from Chu and Ju cited in this book also come from this survey unless indicated otherwise.

2

Chinese Personal Relationship Development Processes

A: I'm so glad that Xiao Mei is going to marry Chen Yuan.

B: Chen Yuan? The youngest son of Mr. Chen?

A: Yes. Mr. Chen has been so good to us over the years. We owe him a lot. Unfortunately, we haven't been able to pay him back.

B: Oh, you don't need to worry about that now. The Chens will be your in-laws. So tell me how this marriage thing came about.

A: You know Xiao Mei and Chen Yuan played together when they were small, but they had their own friends after they started school. About two years ago, they started to have good feelings toward each other and they have been together ever since.

Exchanges such as these are commonly found in various Chinese relational discourses. To Chinese, a sense of indebtedness and repayment of such indebtedness are both important concerns and defining attributes in a person's relational development. Chinese personal relationship development is not only influenced by but also an integral part of the Chinese self-conception. Our understanding of the Chinese self would be incomplete without a close examination of the broader relational context in which the self is situated. Thus, in this chapter, we investigate affective dimensions of Chinese interpersonal relationships. Specifically, we focus on the relational principles of *gan qing* (感情; "feeling"), *ren qing* (人情; "human feeling"), and *bao* (报; "reciprocity"). These three principles represent core dimensions of affective experiences in Chinese interpersonal relationships. They operate in various stages of relationship development processes and are salient concepts in everyday Chinese discourse. We also discuss the implications of *gan qing, ren qing,* and *bao* for affective communication in Chinese culture. The perspective on self and OTHER presented in Chapter 1 provides a conceptual framework for understanding and explaining affective dimensions of Chinese interpersonal relationships.

Moreover, the notion of "other orientation" is important in analyzing and interpreting such issues as how feeling is developed and nurtured as well as how reciprocity is conducted. We begin with *gan qing*—the basis of Chinese personal relationships.

◆ *Gan Qing* (感情; "Feeling"): The Basis of Chinese Personal Relationships

Gan qing is a key affective concept in Chinese culture that bears no English equivalent. The Chinese word *gan qing* does not correspond to the Western notion of "emotions" (Sun, 1991); rather, it symbolizes mutual good feelings, empathy, friendship and support, and love between two people with little emphasis on the sexual aspect. *Gan qing* encompasses a wide array of relational contexts, and, consequently, its meaning may vary from one context to another. For example, *gan qing* between a parent and a child tends to emphasize the components of support, care, and closeness, whereas that between a boyfriend and a girlfriend stresses affection, love, and concern for one another. Mutual good feelings, empathy, and friendship are essential to *gan qing* in friendships.

As a Chinese relational attribute, *gan qing* defines and validates the nature of interpersonal relationships. *You gan qing* (有感情; "having feeling") shows that a relationship has an affective foundation, whereas *mei you gan qing* (没有感情; "not having feeling") indicates that a relationship lacks such a foundation. The presence and absence of *gan qing* thus suggests two qualitatively different types of relationships. Moreover, the quality of any given relationship is further determined by *gan qing* as being good or bad. A happy and satisfying relationship tends to involve *gan qing hao* (感情好; "good feeling"), whereas an unhappy and unsatisfying relationship often is one with *gan qing bu hao* (感情不好 ; "bad feeling").

Chinese entertain the belief that unlike love at first sight, *gan qing* evolves and grows over time. *Gan qing* can be cultivated and nurtured in a relational context by means of *hu xiang bang zhu* (互相帮助; "mutual aid") and *hu xiang guan xin* (互相关心; "mutual care"). Although mutual aid and mutual care are found in personal relationships across cultures, Chinese use them to establish good feelings and love between people as well as to affirm and symbolize relationships (Potter, 1988). Thus, *gan qing,* as an emotional concept, conveys a sense of mutuality and interdependency, which is consistent with and supports the relational and other focus of the Chinese conception of the self. As is known, the Chinese self is defined by relations with others, and the self would be incomplete if it were separated from others. For Chinese, emotional love is mediated through helping and caring for one another; one expresses love by showing care for and helping the other. For example, helping one learn a subject matter, cooking one a meal, running errands, and advising one about weather and health are common ways to initiate a personal relationship and to express love. In personal relationships, whether they are social, romantic, or marital relationships, "the [Chinese] expressive forms that validate the relationship are not enacted in an idiom of emotional love but in an idiom of work and mutual aid" (Potter, 1988, pp. 201-202). Potter continues, noting that "the West has used the capacity to love as the symbolic basis for social relationships; the Chinese have used the capacity to work" (p. 199). The following account given by a Chinese husband regarding the basis of his marriage further demonstrates this approach (Potter, 1988):

> We were on the same team, and we met working together. In 1973, we began to have good feelings for one another. I helped her family, and she helped mine. I helped them to build a house, to weed their plots, and by taking them to the hospital when they were ill. When we were the right age, we registered the marriage. My wife's side did not ask for the little cakes the groom's family is supposed to contribute, but I gave them anyway. (p. 201)

Consequently, *pei yang gan qing* (培养感情 ; "to nurture feeling") becomes the basis for any type of relationship ranging from romantic to friendship (Sun, 1991).

In romantic relationships, the relational orientation of the Chinese self also influences the conception of *gan qing*. Given that family, others, and the surrounding environment are essential to the Chinese self-construal, in Chinese culture a major source of intimacy throughout life comes from a person's bond to the family and in-groups (Hsu, 1970); strong and stable family relations play important roles in a person's life (Chu, 1989). Consequently, Chinese affective experiences such as love often are shared in a broader social context; thus, they are diffused, not highly concentrated within a given relationship, and have low intensity (Dion & Dion, 1988; Hsu, 1981). To a couple, love is often one among other considerations, such as obligations to the parents and family. Research findings are consistent with this assessment. North Americans, for example, report a greater degree of passion in romantic relationships than do their Chinese counterparts. Chinese and North Americans, however, do not differ in their level of intimacy or commitment (Gao, 1993).

The Chinese expression of *gan qing* is embedded in the acts of helping and caring for one another rather than in overt verbal messages. To Chinese, feelings are not to be spoken but to be sensed and discerned. Given the emphasis on implicit understandings of how others feel, discussions of love, for example, often are subtle and indirect (Potter, 1988). In personal relationships, Chinese hardly ever speak of their feelings toward one another. Husband and wife, boyfriend and girlfriend, mother and daughter, and father and son rarely hug or kiss one another in public or private settings. On wedding anniversaries, husbands rarely send wives flowers to symbolize their love (Li, 1986). Compared with people in other cultures, Chinese are not very emotionally expressive, especially in matters regarding sex (Sun, 1991). Chinese tend to view love as an internal feeling that need not be expressed in words because actions have replaced words (Yu & Gu, 1990). Chinese rarely say *wo ai ni* (我爱你; "I love you") to one another; even when one is bold enough to say it, it often makes the hearer feel ill at ease. For many Chinese, such a revelation is almost embarrassing (Yu & Gu, 1990).

Control and moderation further define the appropriate use and expression of *gan qing*. They coincide with and are supported by prevalent Chinese beliefs. To Chinese, self-control of emotional expressions is both a sign of maturity and the basic rule of human interaction. An overwhelming majority of parents in Shanghai and a slight majority of parents in Singapore, for example, endorsed that parents should not display intimacy in the presence of their child (Wu, 1996). Chinese are restrained from stating strong likes and dislikes. Even if they are overwhelmed by someone or something, they often choose to understate their feelings. For example, when Chinese are madly in love with someone, they might say that they "like" the person, whereas when North Americans are in the same situation, they might say that they are "crazy" about the person. Unlike many North Americans, Chinese rarely display or verbalize overt joy, delight, and happiness after receiving a present. Words bearing emotional intensities often reside in literary writings instead of in everyday discourse. Li (1986) cautions that Chinese children who grow up in the United States and see their classmates being constantly kissed and hugged by their parents may misinterpret these actions and believe that their Chinese parents do not love them as much because of the absence of such display of love.

In Chinese culture, *gan qing* is construed not only as an affective issue but also as a health issue. Chinese believe that emotional instability can cause harm to various human organs, and counterbalancing emotions is essential to achieving internal balance and emotional stability (Wu, 1982). Excessive joy, for example, injures the heart but can be counterbalanced by fear, as can grief by joy

(Wu, 1982). In addition, Chinese have learned to express their emotions in terms of bodily organs, such as the heart being the locus of emotions, and consequently, physical conditions rather than emotional states are often cared for (Kleinman, 1980).

The unique notion of *gan qing* and its mode of expression often create misinterpretation, misunderstanding, and confusion in Chinese interactions with others. Lin (1993) suggests that many Chinese women tend to mistake foreigners' (North Americans') friendly expressions, such as being more caring, gentle, romantic, and extroverted, for love. Chinese, however, are perceived to be overwhelming and infringing on others' personal privacy and autonomy when they exhibit constant concern for and attention to others. Many stories are told of Chinese who show concern by telling others to put on some warm clothes when the temperature drops a degree or to take some medicine at the detection of a sneeze but feel frustrated and disheartened because they often are misunderstood; their caring gestures often are (mis)interpreted as signs of encroachment and overstepping. Chinese are also viewed as lacking emotional intensity and focused attention. A lack of expressiveness in Chinese personal relationships creates another set of difficulties. Overt expressions of feelings often make Chinese uncomfortable and awkward, but they are important to those who prize verbal assurance and validation. North Americans, for example, would say, "If you don't tell me you love me, how would I know you do?" Lin (1993) suggests that Chinese who are dating "foreigners" should try not to keep their feelings to themselves and express these to their partners.

To summarize, the relational orientation of the Chinese self explains and supports the Chinese notion of *gan qing*. As the basis of Chinese personal relationships, *gan qing* is achieved primarily through helping and caring for one another, and its expression tends to be subtle and implicit. Chinese emphasize the involvement and participation of others in their affective experiences. Attending and responding to others' needs and wishes provides the foundation for a viable relationship. *Gan qing* is an emotional bond that is mutually constructed, nurtured, and strengthened.

A relationship with *gan qing* is one that values mutuality and interdependence.

◆ *Ren Qing* (人情; "Human Feeling") and *Bao* (报; "Reciprocity")

Given that the Chinese self is defined by relations with others, smooth and harmonious interpersonal transactions become highly critical to a person's self-definition. In Chinese culture, *ren qing* and *bao* represent two important dimensions of Chinese interpersonal transactions. The literal translation of *ren qing* is human feeling. *Ren qing,* however, involves three layers of meanings: feelings between people, a person's natural inclinations, and interpersonal resources (Yang, 1990b). The Chinese word *bao* as a verb has multiple meanings, including "to report," "to respond," "to repay," "to retaliate," and "to retribute" (Yang, 1957). *Bao* takes two forms: The rational *bao* is native Chinese, and the irrational *bao* or fatalism originated in the Indian culture (Wen, 1990).

Ren qing possesses both expressive and instrumental functions (Zhu, 1990). As an affective concept, *ren qing* can be used to express sincere feelings one has toward others. *Ren qing* as interpersonal resources functions as an important mechanism in regulating Chinese personal relationships (Yang, 1990b). A person can give and take *ren qing* as interpersonal resources. Once *ren qing* is presented, one immediately is in a double-bind situation: Rejecting *ren qing* is rude and disruptive to the harmony of the relationship, but accepting it will make one vulnerable to any request for a favor. In Chinese culture, it is expected that one grant the request of the person from whom one has accepted *ren qing.* Despite the inherent perplexity of the *ren qing* rule, Chinese are deeply aware of the social investment value of *ren qing* and thus partake in its ongoing process of give and take.

Chinese self-development is connected closely with the self's orientation to others' needs, wishes, and expectations. This other orientation is also reflected in the notion of *bao*. *Bao* is very important in interpersonal transactions, and it is other oriented.

Bao focuses on repaying the other, and its principle covers many relational spheres (e.g., parent-child relationships, friendships, and work relationships). In modern Chinese societies, *bao* is less collectively oriented (Yang, 1990a). That is, Chinese do not need to pay back the debts their parents or grandparents owed; they are responsible only for paying back their own debts. The investment value of *bao* is also decreasing. *Bao* is considered a relational bond, and expectations of return are not as high. In addition, the obligation to reciprocate is not as strong but is determined by the individual. Finally, the Chinese fatalistic belief is declining. Although the Chinese concept of *bao* is becoming more individually oriented, its impact on personal relationships is still far-reaching (Yang, 1990a). The relational boundaries by which the self is surrounded involve a constant need for reciprocation.

FILIAL PIETY

Xiao (孝; "filial piety") is an indigenous Chinese notion that explicates the "proper" relationship between children and parents. In Chinese culture, a child that observes filial piety is expected to obey the parents and provide for them the needed financial support. For Chinese, the basic virtue of *xiao* finds its justification in the concept of *bao* (Yang, 1957). Sun (1991) contends that

in Chinese culture, a person is motivated to serve and make sacrifices by means of sense of indebtedness. The principle is that a person is already in debit before he [or she] is born; he or she owes a debt to the parents who conceive them, and who will raise them in the future. Indeed, paying back the benevolence of the parents becomes the prototype for all the reciprocal transactions in society. (p. 35)

The importance of filial piety, a special form of *bao,* is perceived to be not incompatible with the "modern" life. Results of recent studies in Hong Kong report that 85% of the respondents want a law to force people to care for elderly parents; 77% would voluntarily and happily support their parents (Wong & Stewart,

1990). In mainland China, Article 49 of the constitution (cited in Wong & Stewart, 1990, p. 530) states, "Parents have the duty to rear and educate their minor children" and "Children who have come of age have the duty to support and assist their parents." A vast majority (80%) of the Chinese respondents in one study indicated that children should look after their parents and parents should ask their children for financial help (Chu & Ju, 1993). Consequently, it is inconceivable for a Chinese person not to feel indebted to parents, family, and friends, as well as to society. The feeling of indebtedness serves as a control mechanism in regulating a Chinese person's behavior.

RECIPROCITY PRINCIPLES

In Chinese personal relationships, *ren qing* and *bao* are often used interchangeably because of their intimate connection. Wang (1990) argues that *ren qing* is the way of managing interpersonal relationships. The notion of *ren qing,* however, is based on the moral code of *bao* (Hsu, 1971; Yang, 1957). A person who *dong ren qing* (懂人情; "understands *ren qing*") knows *bao* ("how to reciprocate"). Chinese culture fosters a strong sense of gratitude and indebtedness; *gan en dai de* (感恩戴德; "bearing a debt of gratitude for one's kindness"), *gan en tu bao* (感恩图报; "feeling grateful for a kind act and planning to repay it"), and *ni jing wo yi chi, wo jing ni yi zhang* (你敬我一尺, 我敬你一丈 ; "you honor me a foot, and I will in return honor you ten feet") are ingrained in the minds of Chinese. Chinese are taught to remember that a person who is indebted to *ren qing* (*qian ren qing*; 欠人情) needs to pay back (*hui bao*; 回报), as exemplified in a well-known Chinese saying, *li shang wang lai* (礼上往来; "reciprocation of greetings, favors, and gifts"). *Li shang wang lai* is perceived as a very important relational value in Chinese culture (Chinese Culture Connection, 1987). A study in Taiwan revealed that the concepts of *ren qing* and *bao* are significant in the informants' accounts of their personal relationships (Chang, 1992). Even in today's China, a large majority of the respondents (82.1%) still endorse the importance of repaying kindness in social relations (Chu & Ju, 1993). The need to reciprocate suggests that relations not only define the Chinese self but also are an integral part of a Chinese person's life.

Given the paramount need to repay one's gratitude in Chinese culture, the principle of reciprocity permeates all types of interpersonal relationships and defines appropriate interpersonal behavior. In social and personal interactions, a Chinese becomes vulnerable or at least feels uneasy to be indebted to someone, and a return is called for to achieve balance in a relationship. For example, if one were given a gift, one would immediately feel compelled to repay the gift in one form or another so as not to owe a debt of gratitude. If one fails to reciprocate, one is perceived as *bu dong ren qing* (不懂人情; "being ignorant of human feeling") or *mei you liang xin* (没有良心; "heartless"). Personal accounts such as "XXX helped me and my family then. We'll do whatever to help XXX now" and "How could you walk away from someone who has been so good to you?" attest to the importance of reciprocity in Chinese personal relationships. Thus, the appropriate use of the principle of reciprocity affects not only the nature and quality of a relationship but also others' perceptions of a person. To Chinese, reciprocity is the basic rule of being a person.

Chinese have the tendency to put family relationships before other types of relationships and to make clear distinctions between insiders and outsiders. Consequently, the nature of a given relationship is essential to the intricate interchange between *ren qing* and *bao* in the everyday life of Chinese; it determines how *ren qing* and *bao* are conceptualized, gauged, and applied. According to Hwang (1987), interpersonal transactions can be viewed and differentiated in the context of the petitioner and the resource allocator. Three types of relationships exist between the petitioner and the resource allocator: expressive tie, mixed tie, and instrumental tie. In an expressive-tie relationship (i.e., between family members), *ren qing* and *bao* are dictated by the rule of "need" and filial piety (Hwang, 1987). Children, for example, are expected to care for their elder parents as a way of repaying their gratitude. When a relationship is based on an instrumental tie, the rule of equity is applied (Hwang, 1987), and reciprocation is often in the form of an impersonal business transaction lacking the dimension of indebtedness (Chang, 1992). A mixed-tie relationship, however, tends to pose the biggest challenge to the appropriate exercise of *ren qing* and *bao*.

As Hwang (1987) notes, a mixed-tie relationship is outside a person's immediate family and not as strong as an expressive-tie relationship. In this relational context, the *ren qing* rule applies (Hwang, 1987). The level of indebtedness one feels toward the other is determined by the scope of *ren qing* (e.g., small or big; Chang, 1992) and the degree of intimacy and closeness of the relationship. Returns are carefully measured to be proportionate to *ren qing* owed (Chang, 1992). The value of one's return of a job offer, for example, should outweigh that of a dinner invitation. In mixed-tie relationships, *guan xi* (关系; "connection") defines how big or small a favor one receives and the size of a return. Consequently, Chinese devote their time and effort to *gao guan xi* (搞关系; "building connections") and *la guan xi* (拉关系; "pulling connections") through doing favors and giving face. When one has an established connection with somebody, one can skillfully employ the principle of *ren qing* and *bao*. In today's China, *guan xi* is still prevalent in many aspects of a person's life, and a vast majority of Chinese perceive connections as important and strongly advocate the use of them (Chu & Ju, 1993).

To summarize, *ren qing* and *bao* are pivotal dimensions of Chinese personal relationships. The giving and receiving of *ren qing* takes place in a reciprocal process and concerns all parties involved. *Ren qing* and *bao* not only characterize the affective aspect of Chinese personal relationships but also accentuate the relational bond one has with others in the Chinese self development. The ability to use *ren qing* and *bao* is thus highly desirable not only in Chinese personal relationships but also in the Chinese self-conception.

◆ Conclusion

In this chapter, we presented two core dimensions in Chinese personal relationship development processes: *gan qing* and *ren qing/bao*. *Gan qing* and *ren qing/bao* are key to our understanding of Chinese affective experiences and the Chinese self-OTHER perspective. The relational and other focus of the Chinese self in a relationship context is reflected in how feeling is constructed and nurtured and in the importance of reciprocity. Attending to others' needs and wishes and involving others in one's affective experiences suggest the critical role others play in a Chinese person's emotional development process. The relational nature of the Chinese self also makes it imperative for Chinese to know how people are connected and how to reciprocate favors.

3

Characteristics of Chinese Communication

A man was interested in a woman whom he met at the new student orientation. He called her up and said "Could we talk? I have something to tell you." So they got together one day. He showed her where he worked and talked extensively about his job, family, and personal interests. Before they parted, he asked, "Do you have a boyfriend?"

In this scenario, both the man and the woman clearly understand the intention of their "get-together," but neither is willing to send a direct and clear verbal message to the other. Scenarios such as this are commonly found in Chinese interpersonal interactions. As a Belgian businessman remarks, "I feel the Chinese never come out directly to tell you their intentions or objectives. Even if there is a conflict, they never try to resolve it in front of you. I feel many Chinese have two faces" (Bi, 1994, p. 69). This Belgian man's experience not only typifies that of many who have come into contact with Chinese but also portrays a style of communication that is associated distinctively with Chinese. How do Chinese communicate? Why do Chinese communicate the way they do? In this chapter, we present some of the characteristics of Chinese communication and examine how those characteristics are conceptualized from the Chinese perspective (i.e., an insider's view). We believe the Chinese way of communicating can be understood, explained, and interpreted only in its cultural context.

Chinese hold many beliefs about talk, and those beliefs, be they implicit or explicit, dictate the daily communicative practices in Chinese culture. One predominant Chinese belief about talk involves the association of speaking with negative consequences as expressed in such adages as *yi yan ji chu, si ma nan zhui* (一言即出,四马难追; "What has been said cannot be unsaid"), *huo cong kou chu* (祸从口出; "Misfortune comes from the mouth"), and *yan duo bi shi* (言多必失; "He [she] who talks errs much"). Speech in Chinese culture thus is constantly exercised with caution and, consequently, perceived as less important (Wiemann, Chen, & Giles, 1986). Chinese often are reminded that if they are not careful about what they say, they will have to deal with various relational and social consequences. It is therefore not surprising for Chinese to use restraint and control in speaking.

Chinese also believe that talk has its limitations and that meanings reside beyond mere words. Expressions such as *yan bu jin yi* (言不尽意; "Not saying all that is felt"), *yan wai zhi yi* (言外之意; "More is meant than meets the ear"), and *zhi ke yi hui, bu ke yan chuan* (只可意会,不可言传; "Can be felt, but not be expressed in words") all emphasize the inadequacy of spoken words in constructing meanings. Hence, the ability to surmise and decipher hidden meanings is highly desirable in Chinese culture.

In addition to the intrinsic beliefs about various implications of talk, the Chinese self-conception and the Chinese personal relationship development processes addressed in previous chapters also influence how Chinese approach communication in their everyday interactions and, consequently, prescribe a set of communication behaviors that are unique to Chinese culture. Given that the Chinese self is defined by relations with others and the self would be incomplete if it were separated from others, the notion of "other" makes up an indispensable part of the Chinese self and permeates all indigenous concepts of Chinese communication. As a result, others' perceptions and views are critical to the interpretation of various messages. Furthermore, maintaining relationships is an integral part of Chinese communication because

Chinese communication is situated in relationships rather than in individual persons, and the primary functions of communication are to maintain existing relationships among individuals, to reinforce role and status differences, and to preserve harmony within the group. In Chinese personal relationships, affective experiences, such as *gan qing* (感情; "feeling") and *ren qing/bao* (人情/报; "human feeling/reciprocity"), also focus on the notions of other and "relations." Attending to others' needs and wishes and involving others in one's affective experiences are essential to the development of *gan qing*. Understanding how people are connected and how to reciprocate favors is the essence of being a model person in Chinese culture.

The previously mentioned Chinese beliefs about talk, the other focus of the Chinese self, and the relation-oriented affective experiences influence speaking practices in everyday lives of Chinese, and specifically, they point to four major characteristics of Chinese communication: (a) *han xu* (含蓄) or implicit communication, (b) *ting hua* (听话) or listening centeredness, (c) *ke qi* (客气) or politeness, and (d) *zi ji ren* (自己人) or a focus on insiders. In the following sections, we examine these characteristics and their applications to understanding Chinese communication.

◆ Han Xu (含蓄; "Implicit Communication")

The Chinese word *han* (含) denotes "to contain," "to embody," and "to reserve." The term *xu* (蓄) means "to store" and "to save." The Chinese phrase *han xu* refers to a mode of communication (both verbal and nonverbal) that is contained, reserved, implicit, and indirect. *Han xu* is considered a social rule in Chinese culture (Yu & Gu, 1990). That is, *han xu* defines appropriate communication in various social and relational contexts. To be *han xu,* one does not spell out everything but leaves the "unspoken" to the listeners.

The practice of *han xu* in Chinese communication is compatible with the conceptualization of self in a relational context. An implicit style of communication enables one to negotiate meanings with others in interpersonal relationships and to help maintain existing relationships among individuals without destroying group harmony. Chinese often say that when there are things left to be said, there often is room for "free advance and retreat." It is not uncommon for two people to have good feelings toward each other, for example, but never express them overtly because both sides fear that direct communication may place them in an unmanageable situation and thus cause damage to their existing relationship.

The notion of *han xu* also fits in with Chinese beliefs about talk. An indirect approach to communication emphasizes what is implied or not said rather than what is said, thus compensating for the inadequacy of spoken words. In Chinese culture, children are taught and encouraged to apply *cha yan guan se* (察言观色; "examining a person's words and observing his [her] countenance") in their communication with others. That is, focusing on *how* something is said, and on what is *not* said is equally, if not more, important than *what* is said. In addition, the rule of *han xu* enables one to utilize a covert style of speaking, thus minimizing the potential misfortune resulting from speaking.

Han xu implies that communication in Chinese culture is inherently negotiable and that the roles of a speaker and a listener are equally important in ongoing communication processes. When Chinese vaguely express an idea, an opinion, or a suggestion, they expect their conversational partner to be highly involved and to take an active role in deciphering messages as well as in mutually creating meanings. A hesitant and indirect approach serves to grant the listener an equal footing with the speaker in a conversation; it further suggests that talk should be collectively carried out and constructed. Talk involves the joint effort of both the speaker and the listener. Young (1994) indicates that a Chinese speaker serves the role of guiding rather than dictating a conversation by employing various skills to suggest and to evoke. In the meantime, "It [the Chinese version of rhetoric] nurtures a tacit and nuanced understanding and defers to the listener's ability to realize its full significance" (Young, 1994, p. 52).

The value of *han xu* also explains the importance of nonverbal communication in Chinese culture. Meanings often reside in unspoken messages. For example, a hand movement, a smile, and a pause convey embedded meanings. Chinese may smile to express embarrassment, frustration, or nervousness. In addition, nonverbal communication often provides important cues for interpretation of verbal messages. Consistent with Hall's (1976) conceptualization of high-context communication, Chinese communication emphasizes the nonverbal more than the verbal aspects of communication.

Han xu involves a lack of expressiveness that is apparent in everyday life of Chinese. Hsu (1971) indicates that Chinese are socialized not to openly express their own personal emotions, especially strong and negative ones. To a Chinese, extreme emotions often are viewed as sources of various health problems, and moderation in emotional expressions is essential to achieving internal balance (Bond, 1993). *The Yellow Emperor's Classic of Internal Medicine* (cited in Bond, 1993) states that "When joy and anger are without moderation, then cold and heat exceed all measure and life is no longer secure" (p. 254).

Empirical observations and research suggest that emotional expressions, such as love, anger, joy, and depression, are covert and contained in Chinese culture. Monitoring overt emotional expression is the basic rule of human interaction. In interpersonal relationships, such as social, romantic, or marital, Chinese rarely verbalize their emotional love, and love is often expressed through caring and helping each other (Potter, 1988). Therefore, unspoken actions, not words, are emphasized in Chinese communication. *Han xu* also influences how joy and anger are expressed. For example, a Chinese person is rarely seen jumping up and down upon receiving a piece of good news. When presented with a gift, Chinese are less likely to display the same level of joy and delight that is characteristic of North Americans. Chinese usually open a gift in private rather than in front of their gift givers. This can be explained by their face-sensitive concern for not "imposing" or "displaying" their feelings inappropriately. Compared with North Americans, Chinese tend to display more reserved and less overt facial expressions even in joyful occasions. Furthermore, Chinese insist that the child should not show feelings of anger, disappointment, or vengeance overtly (Smith, 1991). By not showing joy, sadness, or anger overtly, Chinese avoid imposing their feelings on others to maintain harmony (Bond, 1993; Bond & Hwang, 1986). Support for the existence of *han xu* can be found in cross-cultural and clinical research. Hong Kong Chinese, for example, have more rules about controlling emotional expression in general than do respondents from individualistic cultures (Argyle, Henderson, Bond, Iizuka, & Contarello, 1986). By engaging in laughing and giggling, Chinese show embarrassment, anxiety, nervousness, and social discomfort (Hu & Grove, 1991). In a clinical context, Taiwanese informants are reluctant to reveal their deep and private ideas and feelings. For them, requesting or freely expressing such information is "embarrassing" and "shameful" (Kleinman, 1980). Kleinman suggests that personal ideas, values, and feelings often are conveyed indirectly through descriptions of situations.

Furthermore, *han xu* dictates a style of communication that puts much emphasis on nonverbal behavior and an indirect mode of communication. In the film *Eat Drink Man Woman* (Hsu & Lee, 1994), for example, a retired chef in Taiwan did not know how to talk to his children, but he showed his love by preparing elaborate Sunday dinners for them. Bo (1992) argues that a Chinese may be so hungry that you can hear his or her stomach rumbling, but if you ask that person, "Have you had dinner?" he or she would answer "yes." Thus, observing one's body language and facial expression helps to determine what is on a Chinese person's mind and to understand the true message (Bo, 1992). A Chinese American testified (Himmel, 1996, p. 18), "Growing up we learned: You don't need to say it because if it's true, people will know it [by your actions]." In Chinese culture, *pang qiao ce ji* (旁敲侧击; "beating around the bush") is a skill that nurtures an implicit understanding. Zhang (1994) states that

> I feel Chinese are too *han xu* (implicit). They always talk in a roundabout way and never get to the point. They rarely show their emotions such as happiness or anger and feelings for their parents, siblings, and friends often are buried deep in their hearts. (p. 99)

Chinese also report greater confidence in their ability to predict other people's behavior based on indirect expressions in romantic relationships than do North Americans (Gao & Gudykunst, 1995). That is, Chinese rely more on information that is indirect and nonverbal to reduce their uncertainty about others in personal relationships.

Finally, *han xu* is also an essential quality in Chinese writing. When referring to the ambivalent and equivocal style of Chinese writing, Kaplan (as cited in Young, 1994) remarks that, "Things are developed in terms of what they are *not,* [italics added] rather than what they are" (p. 92). In summary, to Chinese, the most desirable communication practice is to let things speak for themselves (*bu yan er yu;* 不言而喻). In the event that speaking becomes necessary, however, the rule of *han xu* is often elected and favored. Engaging in a direct style of communication with others is the least desirable approach and, consequently, one must bear the burden of being direct.

◆ *Ting Hua* (听话; "Listening-Centeredness")

The speaker and the listener are two of the important components of the communication process.[1] Whereas speakers are defined by what message they send and how they send it, listeners are defined by their ability to understand and interpret the message received. Most communication involves continuous and equalized exchanges between the speaker and the listener. The equilibrium between the speaker and the listener, however, ceases to exist when status and role relationships are the most important attributes of interpersonal interactions.

In Chinese culture, the self involves and is defined by multiple layers of relationships with others. Chinese personal identities are connected closely with the social roles they play. To be sensitive to one's position as above, below, or equal to others (Chu, 1985; Fairbank, 1991; King & Bond, 1985) and ordering relationships by status and observing such order influence how one should perceive oneself in relation to others, how one should develop personal relationships with others, and more important, how one should engage in communication with others. The prominence of status and role relationships in Chinese culture prescribes not only different meanings for the speaker and the listener but also a distinct set of rules of communication. The position one occupies in the hierarchical structure often determines how much one speaks, if at all, and how one speaks. As a result, Chinese communication in the context of status and role relationships is portrayed as listening centered, asymmetrical, and deferential.

To Chinese, there are conditions associated with speaking, and not everyone is entitled to speak. People voice their opinions only when they are recognized. Recognition is often derived from one's expertise on a subject due to years of experience, education, or a power position. Thus, a spoken "voice" is equated with seniority, authority, age, experience, knowledge, and expertise. As a result, listening becomes a predominant mode of communication. For example, the cultural belief that a good child is one who "listens talk" (*ting hua*, 听话) can be found not only in the family context but also in various situations beyond the family. In the Chinese family, children are socialized to take in what their parents say. Obedient children are those who listen but do not voice their own opinions. One often hears parents telling their children *bie cha zui* (别插嘴; "don't interrupt") during family conversations. The ability to listen is therefore highly emphasized as a major mode of communication for children. The rationale that parents are more experienced and have more authority in the family provides support for children's passive mode of communication. Speaking, however, is reserved for parents.

Empirical research provides support for the previously discussed pattern of communication between parents and children. Smith (1991), for example, observed clear roles of communication at the dinner table in Taiwan. The eldest men in the family engage in most of the talking, whereas the children listen and support their elders by occasional comments. The children are to respect but not to challenge their elders (Smith, 1991). When a child challenges a parent verbally or *huan zuei* (还嘴; "talks back"), it is considered disobedient behavior and harmony in the family is disrupted. The adoption of an asymmetrical style of communication, reflecting core Confucian values, serves to maintain the existing status and role relationships in Chinese culture. The hierarchical structure in the family and role differentiation are created and reinforced when parents engage in more talking and children in more listening. Similar asymmetrical patterns of communication exist for other relationships as well. For example, students are expected to listen to their teachers the majority of the time. They are there to hear what the esteemed teachers have to say. Most Chinese schools emphasize listening skills, memorizing skills, writing skills, and reading skills but rarely emphasize speaking skills. As a result, Chinese children have poor verbal fluency because assertiveness and eloquence are considered signs of disrespect (Liu, 1986). The previous assessment is consistent with research findings. Chinese children, for example, scored higher on reasoning, number facility, and space conceptualization than black and Puerto Rican children, but their verbal ability was lower than that of Jewish and black children (Lesser, 1976; Lesser, Fifer, & Clark, 1965).

This role pattern of superior speaking and inferior listening also extends to work relationships. A good employee, for example, is one who listens to talk (*tin hua*), does what he or she is told, and has the willingness to meet others' expectations and accept others' criticism (Zhuang, 1990). In most work situations, communication interaction means learning to listen and, most important, learning to listen with full attention. Feedback is often limited if not totally absent. Given that the ability to listen is stressed, promoted, and rewarded in the context of hierarchy and role relationships, Chinese constantly seek to cultivate and refine their listening skills. As a result, they are more likely to detect any nuance and subtlety embedded in verbal messages.

The focus on listening supports the nonconfrontational way of life in Chinese culture. That is, when people engage in talk, argumentation or questioning is often an inseparable part of the process. When people focus on listening, however, direct confrontations as such can be avoided. The importance of listening is also consistent with a commonly held cultural belief that the mouth (i.e., spoken words) is the root of many misfortunes and calamities in interpersonal interactions. Research on business communication provides further support for this conception. Chinese managers rank the oral communication skill as the least important in their preparation for the position (Hildebrandt, 1988). Hildebrandt attributes such lack of perceived need for oral communication to the Chinese managerial system, which promotes acceptance but not assertiveness, argumentation, or debate. Feedback and challenging, questioning, and interrupting others tend to be reduced or absent in Chinese managerial meetings compared with North American ones (Lindsay & Dempsey, 1985). In addition, given that communication is implicit and indirect in Chinese culture, message interpretation by the listener becomes highly important. Yum (1991) argues that communication in Asian cultures is receiver centered.

Respect for authority and status differences are reflected not only in the focus on listening but also in the use of a deferential style of communication. To be deferential, one needs to exercise both restraint and hesitance in the presence of authority (Young, 1994). For example, even if one feels nothing but certain, assured, and definite about an idea or a suggestion, one should phrase it in a tentative and hesitant manner so as not to question the authority or pose a threat to the authority. This orientation is aptly stated by one Chinese respondent (Young, 1994):

> Your idea, you should not be sure your idea is correct. . . . Even though your idea is good, you don't know how the boss will think. . . . Even if he [the subordinate] is confident enough to present this correct idea, he does not want to hurt the authority of the boss. He still has to give room to the boss to consider. (p. 154)

How then do Chinese apply restraint and hesitance in their communication with authority figures? Two approaches are commonly adopted by the subordinate. First, the subordinate needs to appear conciliatory and agreeable to show deference and honor.

Second, the subordinate needs to downplay the significance of a point by using such phrases as "I think," "I'm not sure," and "I don't know." To present oneself as agreeable and provisional is imperative in the public presence of authority, as exemplified in Silin's (as cited in Young, 1994) observation of communication between the boss and the employee in a Taiwanese organization:

> To publicly express alternative ideas is to express lack of confidence in the boss. Such expressions are ultimately threatening to his [her] position as chief, and at least vaguely, disrespectful. Individuals who hold such ideas are assumed to harbor personal, egocentric, and antigroup ambitions. (p. 150)

In short, status and role relationships are instrumental in shaping the way people communicate in Chinese culture. As a focal point of Chinese communication, listening has redefined the role of the speaker and that of the listener. King and Bond (1985) suggest that this type of communication is nonreciprocal and passive. It can be argued, however, that Chinese communication appears to be "passive" in speaking, but it emphasizes "activeness" in listening. Thus, it is essential for a speaker to have the ability to determine if a message is received or accepted or both by listeners through various means, such as detecting nonverbal cues and second-guessing.

◆ *Ke Qi* (客气; "Politeness")

Ke qi (politeness) is a basic principle that Chinese observe in their everyday speaking practices. The notion of *ke qi* delineates that communication between the self and others should be construed in a thoughtful, mannerly, pleasant, and civil fashion. Given that the Chinese self needs to be defined, recognized, and completed by others, seeking harmony with others and preserving peaceful relations with others becomes a primary task in a person's relational development and interpersonal communication. Thus, engaging in *ke qi* interactions is necessary for Chinese to accomplish their relational goals.

Grounded in the Chinese relational concept of self and concern for others, the ritual of *ke qi* applies to all interpersonal interactions and concerns all parties involved. In general, amicable and congenial interpersonal relationships are based on a balanced exchange of polite talk. To show respect and deference to authority, for example, Chinese children are taught to engage in polite talk with parents and other elders. The ritual of *ke qi,* however, is most preeminent in the Chinese host-guest context.

In the host-guest relationship, the host demonstrates *ke qi* by doing everything to make the guest "feel at home," and the guest returns *ke qi* by not imposing on the host. This process of polite interaction is typical in Chinese culture. For example, a Chinese person's first response to any offer, ranging from a cup of tea to a dinner invitation, is often the ritualized "no." *No* here does not symbolize a rude rejection as conceptualized in some cultures or "self-denial" (Schneider, 1985); rather, it is an expression of politeness. The host, however, is expected to insist until the offer is accepted. By not accepting the guest's expressed wishes at face value, the host demonstrates the "sincerity" of the offer (Wierzbicka, 1996). Chen (1991) observes this type of ongoing exchange of politeness at the Chinese dinner table. The ritual of *ke qi* (i.e., offer-decline-offer-decline-offer-accept) defines most Chinese host-guest interactions.

Although the "offer-decline" ritual is essential to host-guest interactions, when used in the context of close relationships, especially family relationships, it can be perceived and interpreted as insincere, distant, and removed. Hence, a different set of rules pertains to members of the in-group, and it serves to stress the distinction that exists between insiders and outsiders as well as to accentuate in-group closeness and solidarity. Husbands and wives, for example, do not partake in the *ke qi* ritual, and expressed wishes by in-group members are often accepted at face value. Among in-group members, polite expressions, such as "thank you," "excuse me," and "I'm sorry," are rarely spoken but are internalized. Consequently, observance of *ke qi* has bearing only on interactions involving out-group members, but it can be and has been utilized in Chinese culture as both an interpersonal and a rhetorical device to communicate in-group inclusion or exclusion. That is, a person can choose not to apply the ritual of *ke qi* with an out-group member to show inclusion or a person can insist on observing *ke qi* with an in-group member to show exclusion. This will be discussed further under the section "The Insider Effect on Communication."

Ke qi also embodies the values of modesty and humbleness in Chinese culture. To grow up as a Chinese, one learns not to take credit for one's behavior or be boastful in any situation. To understate one's ability, expertise, strength, or competence and to engage in self-effacing talk are an integral part of the Chinese socialization process. Terms such as *yu jian* (愚见; "stupid opinion"), *zhuo zuo* (拙作; "clumsy work"), *han she* (寒舍; "shabby house"), and *bi xiao* (敝校; "humble school") are utilized to be self-directed, whereas *gao jian* (高见; "great opinion"), *da zuo* (大作; "big work"), *gui fu* (贵府; "precious mansion"), and *gui xiao* (贵校; "precious school") are other-directed (Y. G. Gu, 1990). When receiving a compliment, for example, a Chinese would employ the ritual of *ke qi* and automatically say the phrase, *bu hao, bu hao* (不好不好; "not good") or不好 *na li, na li* (哪里 哪里; "where?" meaning "not really") and be apologetic. To blatantly accept a compliment is considered impolite. This protocol, when applied to interactions with people from other cultures, has the potential for cross-cultural misunderstandings to occur. To North Americans, for example, the cultural norm is to "accept" compliments (Wierzbicka, 1996).

To be modest, Chinese are less likely to display pride in their successful endeavors than are North Americans (Stipek, Weiner, & Li, 1989). Hong Kong Chinese, for example, like self-effacing people more than self-enhancing people, even though self-enhancing people are perceived as more competent (Bond, Leung, & Wan, 1982). This suggests that liking and competence are two separate issues in Chinese culture, even though a connection between liking and competence clearly exists in the United States (Tetlock, 1980). Modesty training not only is an integral part of child education in

Chinese culture but also is adopted by overseas Chinese. One such Chinese American remarked (Himmel, 1996), "If someone says, 'Oh, you're a wonderful person,' your response is, 'Not really.' You don't say 'thank you' to a compliment. You downplay your own importance" (p. 18). Modesty is practiced or remembered or both as an enduring Chinese attribute.

The virtue of Chinese modesty when overdone can create problems for both Chinese themselves and others. Zhang (1994) notes that when other people are capable of doing something, they will say so. Chinese, however, will say they cannot do something even when they can. For example, when an experienced mathematics teacher is asked to give a lecture to a group of people, the most likely response one receives is "I cannot do it." This orientation is destined to create misunderstandings and misconceptions of Chinese. In short, *ke qi* is a recurrent theme in Chinese talk. For Chinese, observance of *ke qi* is not only a self-presentational goal but also a skill essential to any type of interpersonal interaction.

◆ The Insider Effect on Communication

> They [Americans] interact with Asians socially as well as at work and find them to be among the kindest, most considerate, and polite people they have ever met. Then, they meet other Asians in a public situation (on a bus, driving in traffic, in the market) and see them as rude, impolite, and inconsiderate. They wonder how people from the same culture can behave so differently. (Wallach & Metcalf, 1995, p. 161)

The feeling of bewilderment, confusion, and frustration expressed in the previous observation characterizes the experience of many who come from cultures that do not emphasize the distinction between in-groups and out-groups, and whose behavior remains the same regardless of the in-group or out-group situation. In Chinese and other collectivistic cultures, however, the notion of in-group is very significant because in-groups often serve as the primary, ongoing units of socialization of each person. The needs, goals, and beliefs of the in-group often precede those of the individual (Triandis, 1988).

Zi ji ren (自己人; "insider") and *wai ren* (外人; "outsider") are two of the most frequently used concepts in Chinese conversations. Chinese make clear distinctions between insiders and outsiders. A person with an insider status often enjoys privileges and special treatment beyond an outsider's comprehension. Moreover, Chinese are less likely to initiate interactions or to be involved in social relationships with outsiders. Thus, understanding the distinction between an insider and an outsider is an essential task in the Chinese self's relational development. Chinese need to recognize not only where they are in relation to others but also, more important, whether their relationships with others are situated in an in-group or out-group context. The notions of insiders and outsiders are an integral part of the Chinese self-conception.

In the Chinese family unit, insiders include members of the family and relatives. Friends and others with whom one has established a special relationship are considered insiders in a social circle. Insiders in organizations may consist of people on the same hierarchical level, such as members of the production group and members of the supervisors' group. The distinction between an outsider and an insider not only places people in different relational circles but also prescribes specific rules of interaction in communication. Thus, there is not a permeable system of communication in Chinese culture (Barnett, 1979).

The in-group/out-group system of communication can create enormous difficulty for Chinese in interactions with strangers (outsiders) because most Chinese do not feel comfortable or knowledgeable about dealing with strangers. Consequently, interactions with strangers are often initiated by a third person (an intermediary) who is known to both parties (King & Bond, 1985). With the help of an intermediary, unpredictability, even indifference, between outsiders can be reduced. Chinese intermediaries often are close friends of both parties. Close friends are chosen to be mediators because an outsider could not persuade each party to accommodate without a loss of face (Bond, 1991). Also, "A '*wai-ren*'[outsider] would not know what has happened. The two in conflict won't talk about their conflict to a *wai-ren*" (Ma, 1992, p. 274).

The insider effect also influences many other aspects of communication in Chinese culture. It creates a communication context in which outsiders are excluded. Chinese tend to become highly involved in conversations with someone they know (insiders), but they rarely speak to strangers (who are perceived as outsiders). Graf (1994) observes that "Chinese often are perceived to be polite. In reality, they are only polite to those whom they know or have relations with, but indifferent to others" (p. 232). Strangers often do not talk to each other when waiting in a line, on an airplane, or at a social function. Students from Hong Kong and Taiwan self-disclose more to in-group than to out-group members, but no difference in disclosure is found with students from the United States and Australia (Gudykunst et al., 1992). Thus, Chinese are sometimes perceived as cold and distant to strangers (Bo, 1992).

The insider effect suggests that the type of a relationship is a critical dimension in Chinese communication processes. The nature of a relationship determines what is communicated and how information should be communicated. A Chinese cultural expectation is that insiders and outsiders should not be treated in the same way because insiders share a sense of unity and interdependence (Wierzbicka, 1996). The Chinese expression, *bu yao jian wai* (不要见外; "Do not treat yourself as a stranger"), implies the underlying assumption and expectation associated with the notion of a stranger. For example, communication with insiders can be very personal, but with outsiders it can be very impersonal. Compared with North Americans, Chinese are more likely to pursue a conflict with a stranger than with a friend (Leung, 1988). Chinese view lying to strangers as significantly less wrong than do their Canadian counterparts (McLeod & Carment, 1987). In close relationships, especially family relationships, imperative requests are more appropriate, but interrogative requests are expected to be used with others (Wierzbicka, 1996).

Moreover, Chinese are more likely to express feelings and emotions with family members than with nonfamily members

(Chu & Ju, 1993) and with close friends than with acquaintances or strangers (Schneider, 1985). A survey by Chu and Ju (1993) shows that Chinese consult with and are consulted by nonfamily members about work the most (43.9%) and about marriage and family issues the least (12.9%), suggesting that less intimate topics are shared with nonfamily members. Chinese managers tend to deal with problem workers by asking them to have "heart-to-heart" conversations with their coworkers, friends, and family (Krone, Garrett, & Chen, 1992). These intermediaries are expected to influence the "difficult" party to be more amenable. Similar processes are reportedly used in many other similar situations. Research also suggests that Hong Kong Chinese demonstrate more direct resistance to a group insult in the out-group situation than in the in-group or the private situation. With regard to a personal insult, there is less direct resistance in the in-group condition than in the out-group or the private condition (Bond & Venus, 1991). The need to protect the image of the in-group, or the self, is heightened in the presence of the out-group.[2]

In summary, the demarcation between the in-group and the out-group delineates one set of rules of communication for insiders and another for outsiders. The appropriateness of any communication thus depends on the in-group versus the out-group context. That is, approaches contributing to the in-group cohesion and harmony are adopted in communication with insiders, whereas those underscoring the difference between the in-group and the out-group are employed with outsiders. Consequently, the communicative experience with insiders differs vastly from that with outsiders.

◆ Conclusion

In this chapter, we have described Chinese communication processes by identifying several characteristics that guide a Chinese person's communication with others. Specifically, they are (a) *han xu* or implicit communication, (b) *ting hua* or listening-centeredness, (c) *ke qi* or politeness, and (d) *zi ji ren* or a focus on insiders. These characteristics are situated in Chinese beliefs about talk, the relational definition of the self, and Chinese role relationships. Consequently, Chinese communication has an affective focus and is used to affirm a relational identity. We believe that the previously mentioned rules governing appropriate or inappropriate communication practices serve fewer instrumental but rather more affective purposes in Chinese culture.

Notes

1. The distinction between the speaker and the listener is artificial but necessary to make our point clear.

2. One study appears to be inconsistent with the current argument regarding the insider effect. Ma's (1990) study of discontented responses in North American and Chinese relationships reported that type of relationship (intimate, acquaintance, and stranger) did not have an impact on the discontented responses in the Chinese sample. The small sample size ($N = 20$) and the use of a Chinese student sample in the United States may help explain this unexpected result. The inconsistent finding warrants further research on the insider effect on communication.

4

Mian Zi (面子)

Many of us have experienced feelings of pride and elation as well
as those of embarrassment, shame, and humiliation. In Chinese
culture, most of these feelings come directly from gaining or losing
mian zi. The concern for *mian zi* is an integral part of Chinese
self-construal, Chinese personal relationship development, Chinese discourse, and Chinese communication strategies. The prominence of *mian zi* in Chinese culture is insurmountable. In this
chapter, we first present the current conceptualization of *mian
zi*. We then examine various implications of the concern for *mian
zi* in Chinese culture. Finally, we delineate five specific strategies
that exemplify the importance of face concern in Chinese communication.

◆ The Conceptualization of *Mian Zi*

The Chinese term *mian zi* is not widely used in past or current
literature; rather, the concepts of *face* and *facework* are found in
most studies that deal with the issue of self-presentation. *Face*
refers to an individual's claimed sense of positive image in a
relational and network context, and *facework* involves communicative strategies that are used to enact self-face and to uphold,
support, or challenge the other person's face (Ting-Toomey, 1985,

1988). Ting-Toomey argues that both face and facework address projected self-respect and other-consideration issues. People in all cultures try to maintain and negotiate face in all communicative situations, and the concept of face is especially problematic in uncertainty situations (such as request, embarrassment, or conflict situations) when the situated identities of the communicators are called into question (Ting-Toomey, 1988). "Saving face" and "losing face" are two dimensions of face.

In addition to Ting-Toomey's work on face, several other approaches have been developed throughout the years (Brown & Levinson, 1987; Cupach & Metts, 1994; Goffman, 1955; Ho, 1976; Hu, 1944; Lim, 1994; Lim & Bowers, 1991). One approach specifically addresses the issue of face contents (Lim & Bowers, 1991). Lim and Bowers propose that all human beings have three distinct face wants: (a) autonomy face (i.e., the want not to be imposed on), (b) fellowship face (i.e., the want to be included), and (c) competence face (i.e., the want that their abilities be respected). Different types of face want promote the use of different facework strategies.

People in individualistic and collectivistic cultures assign different meanings to the content notions of face. Individualists tend to emphasize nonimposition by others, noninclusion of others, and self-presentational facework competence. In comparison, collectivists tend to emphasize nonimposition of self on others, inclusion of others, and other-directed facework competence. In individualistic cultures, face is associated mostly with self-worth, self-presentation, and self-value, whereas in collectivistic cultures face is concerned more about what others think of one's worth, especially in the context of one's in-group and out-group, than about oneself. In collectivistic cultures, face means projected social image and social self-respect. More specifically, in Chinese culture, gaining and losing face is connected closely with issues of social pride, honor, dignity, insult, shame, disgrace, humility, trust, mistrust, respect, and prestige.

Loose and tight social structures also influence how face is conceptualized. A tight social structure refers to "the extent members of a culture (a) agree about what constitutes correct action,

(b) must behave exactly according to the norms of the culture, and (c) suffer or offer severe criticism for even slight deviations from norms" (Pelto as cited in Triandis, 1995, p. 52). A wide latitude for deviation and variation, however, exists in a culture that has a loose social structure. Consequently, a "face-losing" act is more likely to be stigmatized and to bring disgrace and humiliation to a person in a culture with a tight social structure than in a culture with a loose social structure.

In Chinese culture, the notion of face is embedded in two Chinese concepts: *lian* (脸) and *mian* (面) or *mian zi* (面子). The literal translation of *lian* is "face," whereas "image" serves as an equivalent of *mian zi*. Hu (1944) defines *lian* as something that "represents the confidence of society in the integrity of ego's moral character, the loss of which makes it impossible for him [or her] to function properly within the community" (p. 45). *Lian,* Hu notes, "is both a social sanction for enforcing moral standards and an internalized sanction" (p. 45). *Mian* or *mian zi,* however, "stands for the kind of prestige that is emphasized in [the United States]: A reputation achieved through getting on in life, through success and ostentation" (p. 45). In other words, this definition of *mian zi* corresponds more closely to that of face found in both past and current literature. Consistent with Hu's distinction, King and Myers (1977) view *mian zi* as social or positional face and *lian* as a moral face. Having or not having *mian zi* is externalized and conditioned by how successful one is in meeting established social rules, whereas *lian* tends to be internalized.

In Chinese discourse, the concepts of *lian* and *mian zi* evoke very different meanings. For example, *lian* is often associated with aspects of personal integrity and the moral character of a person and is used in its negative form *bu yao lian* (不要脸; "no face need," meaning shameless) (Gao, in press). The expression *bu yao lian* is a specific and direct condemnation of one's personal integrity and moral character that often has a very negative connotation in Chinese culture. To Chinese, *you lian* (有脸; "to have face") is essential to being a human. It is, however, the loss of *lian* that endures serious consequences in various aspects of a person's life. The loss of *lian* often brings shame or disgrace not only to the person but also to his or her family (Gao, in press). The concept of *mian zi,* however, is not entangled with issues of moral character and personal integrity. The expression *bu yao mian zi* (不要面子; "no image need") suggests one's lack of consideration for public image, which can be interpreted as being "down to earth."

Although there is a pronounced distinction between the use of *lian* (face) and *mian zi* (image) in Chinese discourse, it is important to point out that the concepts of *lian* and *mian zi* can be and have been used interchangeably in some communication contexts in which neither a person's moral character nor personal integrity is implicated. For example, when we are complimented for a job well done, our *lian* or *mian zi* is augmented and enhanced. More research, however, is needed to reveal in what contexts these two concepts convey similar messages and in what contexts they evoke very different ones.

In summary, face is a concept that has been widely researched in both past and current literature. Its conceptualization includes (a) a sense of one's social self-worth or others' assessments of our social "worthiness" or both and (b) a vulnerable resource in social interactions given that it can be threatened, attacked, maintained, and enhanced. In Chinese culture, the notion of face is expressed in *lian* and *mian zi*. The concept of *lian* embodies a moral dimension and often is internalized, whereas *mian zi* signifies a social image and often is externalized.

◆ Implications of the Concern for *Mian Zi*

    A: Are you going to see that show on Saturday?
    B: I'm afraid not. Because I was invited to a piano recital.
    A: I thought you didn't like that kind of music.
    B: It's true, but I feel I need to show up to give my friend *mian zi.*

This conversation typifies many that occur in the everyday Chinese discourse. It illustrates the importance of the concern for *mian zi* in Chinese culture. As a pervasive concept, *mian zi* influences how we perceive ourselves, how we relate to others, and how we speak to others. It is central to the Chinese self-conception and relational development.

In Chinese culture, a person's self-concept is connected closely with one's *mian zi*. Yu and Gu (1990) contend that *mian zi* and social self-esteem are mixed together. *Ren yao lian; shu yao pi* (人要脸, 树要皮 ; "A person needs face like a tree needs bark") is an expression commonly used by Chinese to show such interconnection between one's self-concept and one's projected image in public. The recognition, acceptance, and enhancement of one's self-worth, to a large extent, depends on whether one does or does not have *mian zi*. People in prestigious positions, for example, often are perceived to have *mian zi*, and consequently, their self-worth is enhanced greatly. One's self-worth is also gauged by the size of *mian zi*. A big *mian zi* provides a greater enhancement of one's self-worth compared with a small *mian zi*. Moreover, given that the Chinese self is other oriented and relational in nature and that Chinese self-development is associated closely with the self's orientation to others' needs, wishes, and expectations, the notion of "other" also defines *mian zi*. In Chinese culture, a person's social self-esteem often is formed on the basis of others' remarks. If others' remarks are positive, one's social self-esteem is boosted, and consequently, one has face (Yu & Gu, 1990). As Ting-Toomey (1988) asserts, members of collectivistic cultures are oriented to other-face concern and "we-identity" needs (see also Chang & Holt, 1994; Scollon & Scollon, 1995).

The impact of *mian zi* can be seen in many aspects of a Chinese person's life. In a study of middle-level business executives in Hong Kong, Redding and Ng (1982) found that having face is believed to influence success in business transactions and negotiations. To be given face during a transaction is perceived as highly favorable, whereas to challenge or to destroy face deliberately is viewed as highly unfavorable. Gaining and losing face also influences the affective state of a person. Strong feelings of satisfaction, pride, and enhanced confidence are associated with gaining face, whereas strong negative feelings of shame, worry, uneasiness, anxiety, and tension; difficulty in concentrating on work; and symptoms such as blushing are related to losing face (Redding & Ng, 1982).

Chinese also employ *mian zi* as social capital to make requests and to gain compliance. As social capital, face "can be either 'thick' or 'thin,' weighed, contested, borrowed, given, augmented, diminished" (Young, 1994, p. 19). When one's face is put forth in the formulation of a request, rejection is less likely to occur. Consider the following example: "Xiao Geng has helped me a lot for the last 2 years. To give me *mian zi,* would you please do him this favor?" (Gao, in press). The employment of one's face in making a request is also evident in the following account (Redding & Ng, 1982):

> I telephone them to ask them to give me face by attending the seminar. We Chinese usually say 'please give me face and honor us with your presence.' . . . I also arrange the front seats for the more important companies' representatives as a gesture of giving them more face than others. (p. 212)

The nature of a relationship also determines whether *mian zi* should be given or be contested. It is often more difficult to contest the *mian zi* of a familiar one than that of an unfamiliar one, as demonstrated in the following respondent's narrative (Redding & Ng, 1982): "Recently, a secretary introduced her younger brother into my department. He is not the type of subordinate I want, but I took him only because I had to give face to his sister" (p. 212).

Chiang (1989) argues that the Chinese tradition is more concerned with face than credibility, and Chinese would be most likely to sacrifice "confidence building" for the sake of "face-saving." A well-known Chinese expression, *da zhong lian chong pang zi* (打肿脸充胖子; "to make your face swell to pretend that you are a fat man"), attests to the truth of Chiang's argument. To save face, Chinese are inclined to engage in exaggerated, magnified, and highly colored discourse. For example, a Chinese would portray a strained relationship as one that is happy and satisfying. Chinese would say "yes" to something that they disagree with. To Chinese, as Bond and Lee (1981) argue, protecting another person's face is more important than one's belief of truth or correctness, one's own image, or the risk of being misjudged by others as "uncritical" or "partial." "To put up a front and pretend to be what they are not" (Chiang, 1989, p. 14) characterizes the Chinese "*mian zi* syndrome." Numerous stories have been told about Chinese families that cannot afford to give elaborate and flashy wedding banquets but insist on doing so just to impress others. *Mian zi* syndrome can indeed create its own set of problems.

One's concern for face also governs what one does and does not disclose in personal relationships. Clear boundaries of self-disclosure exist in Chinese culture as demonstrated in the expression *jia chou bu ke wai yang* (家丑不可外扬; "Family disgrace should not be revealed to the outsider"). To avoid the threat of losing face, Chinese tend to not reveal their personal or family disgrace to others. Incidents of misbehavior or wrongdoing are often concealed. As a result, one rarely hears a Chinese person discuss topics such as a dysfunctional family, poor relationships between parents, or sibling rivalry. Various face-saving strategies thus operate in Chinese relationships to protect the need for face.

Furthermore, "face want" serves to regulate a person's behavior. Engaging in appropriate behavior is of concern to most Chinese, especially those whose selves are other oriented and relationally defined. In Chinese culture, inappropriate behavior often results in others' negative remarks and thus brings a loss of face to the person. Acting appropriately entails a prudent consideration of any potential consequences of one's behavior. For example, if one initiates a relationship, then termination becomes a face-threatening act for the initiator. The concern for face influences not only relationship initiation but also its development and deterioration. Hence, the importance of face want has a controlling effect on Chinese behavior. Smith (1991), for example, observes that Chinese families in modern Taiwan constantly evaluate their behaviors because public ridicule in child-rearing practices, in husband-wife relationships, and in caring for the elderly can provoke a loss of face in the family.

In Chinese culture, one's concern for *mian zi* is not only personally based but also collectively based (King & Bond, 1985). As King and Myers (1977) argue, face is more a concern to the family than to the person, and face-losing or face-gaining acts reflect both on persons themselves and on their families. For example, one's failure threatens the face of the family, whereas one's accomplishment gains face for the family. Parents' *mian zi* is enhanced and augmented when their child is successful and is complimented for a job well done. Parents' *mian zi* is attacked and diminished, however, when their child's behavior is condemned. Therefore, Chinese parents often teach their children to behave appropriately by saying *bie diu zan jia de lian* (别丢咱家的脸 ; "Don't make our family lose face").

In summary, *mian zi* is an indispensable concept in Chinese culture. It influences how Chinese perceive themselves, relate to others, and communicate with others. As Young (1994) argues, "Face goes deep to the core of a Chinese person's identity and integrity" (p. 19). Our knowledge and understanding of the conception and implications of *mian zi* will facilitate our future interaction with Chinese.

◆ *Mian Zi* (面子 ; "Face-Directed Communication Strategies")

Concern for *mian zi* significantly influences many aspects of Chinese communication processes (Bond & Lee, 1981; Gao, in press; Wierzbicka, 1996). One important aspect of Chinese communication processes involves the use of communication strategies in personal interactions. Face concern not only explains but also influences the appropriate use of various communication strategies in Chinese culture. Strategies such as nonconfrontation, compliance strategies, provisional responses, using intermediaries, and *yi lun* (议论 ; "to gossip") exemplify the importance of *mian zi* in Chinese communication.

NONCONFRONTATION

Chinese tend to regard conflict and confrontation as unpleasant and undesirable. Ting-Toomey (1988) defines conflict as a problematic situation in which two interdependent parties perceive or have incompatible needs or goals. Conflict requires active face work management (i.e., understanding others' face needs and negotiating face with others). In Chinese culture, conflict is something that most people will avoid at all costs because it invites direct confrontation. Bond (1991) indicates that any direct confrontation or initiation of any type of dispute is considered an invitation to *luan* (乱; "chaos") for Chinese. Chinese do not like chaos because it disrupts the harmonious fabric of personal relationships. Smith (1991) observes that conflicts endanger good relationships between relatives, friends, neighbors, or acquaintances. When the parents of two families are involved in a conflict situation, for example, the children stop playing together and vice versa.

Chinese cherish and nurture the belief that conflict should be approached with self-control and self-restraint. This belief is deeply ingrained in the Chinese psyche. When asked what they would do if they had a quarrel with a neighbor and received verbal abuse, more than half of the Chinese respondents indicated that they would exercise verbal control, and one third indicated that they would go to a neighborhood committee for a settlement (Chu & Ju, 1993). In addition, more than half of the Chinese respondents would prefer means such as "not say anything," "ask the leader to mediate," and "ask a third person" to a direct approach if they experienced a difference of opinion with someone in the work unit (Chu & Ju, 1993). Overall, most Chinese endorse avoidance and other indirect approaches to conflict situations. Even in highly confrontational situations, a Chinese social rule does not support the total demolition of others' public image; rather, it demands that face must be left or *liu mian zi* (留面子).

In cross-cultural analyses, conflict management styles are linked closely to one's concern for face. Three face concerns have been identified: self-face, other face, and mutual face (Ting-Toomey, 1988). Ting-Toomey argues that people in collectivistic cultures are more concerned with other face compared with those in individualistic cultures. Concern for other face often leads to a nonconfrontational style of conflict management, such as avoiding, obliging, and compromising. Mainland Chinese and Taiwanese report a higher degree of obliging and avoiding styles of conflict management than do their U.S. counterparts (Ting-Toomey et al., 1991). That is, the relational self either avoids face-threatening situations or seeks some type of compromise so as not to make the interdependent parties lose face. This strategy of conflict management not only enables both parties to preserve harmony but also helps affirm the relational identity of the self. When relationships are "intact," the self does not lose because "one can be serving oneself as one serves others" (Bond, 1993, p. 256).

Criticism is a predominant domain of conflict that requires care and prudence because of its implications for face. It is often not easy to achieve the delicate balance between face and criticism, as described by one U.S. returnee trained in Chomskyan linguistics (Redding & Ng, 1982): "When I work with my colleagues, I have to be extra careful about how I mix professional comments with considerations of their face. This can be frustrating" (p. 217). In Chinese culture, criticism is often perceived as affectively based and relational in nature. This perception coincides with the belief that ideas are not materials for discussion, validation, interpretation, or evaluation. Young (1994) contends that "Chinese regard one's ideas as entangled with one's identity or sense of personal worth; an attack on one's ideas is therefore an attack on one's self, or, more specifically, one's face" (p. 125).

Therefore, unless it can be avoided, criticism must be approached in an indirect manner. To construct and present criticism in a nonthreatening, face-saving, and gentle manner is a highly desirable interpersonal skill. Hedging strategies, such as (a) disqualifying oneself as a competent critic, (b) using an indirect approach, and (c) making many references to the virtues and skills of the superior before giving criticism, are essential to fulfilling the job and, concurrently, to protecting the face of those who are criticized

(Bond & Lee, 1981). For example, consider the following insightful observation from a retired head of an academic institute in China (Young, 1994):

> Chinese generally try to avoid direct confrontation, try not to make the other person look bad. So they often look for points on which there might be agreement or similarity, even if the other person is thought to be ninety-nine percent wrong. This might be considered a manifestation of the "live and let live" philosophy. By so doing, you are also protecting yourself because in your own arguments or writings you may not be one hundred percent correct. You would wish these to be pointed out in a nonhumiliating face-saving way. (p. 125)

COMPLIANCE STRATEGIES

One's concern for face also affects how disagreements or arguments are handled in a relational context. To "give others face" requires one not to argue or disagree overtly with others in public, especially in the presence of a superior. Thus, for Chinese, meanings in messages cannot be negotiated in public. To negotiate conceivable meanings in public is to question the authority and threaten interpersonal harmony. In business negotiations, for example, any proposal-counterproposal style of negotiating is avoided (Hellweg, Samovar, & Skow, 1991). To Chinese, public disagreement is a face-losing act. Consequently, when one is unavoidably involved in an argument with a friend, it becomes difficult for them to remain friends. To protect face and to preserve interpersonal harmony, as well as the cohesion of the group, Chinese tend to adopt an unassertive style of communication in interpersonal interactions. Chinese have learned to be strategically unassertive by articulating their intentions in an indirect manner and leaving room for negotiations in private. This style of communication not only enables them to accomplish their own agenda but also creates an amicable climate for future cooperation and negotiation. In Chinese culture, assertiveness does not have the positive connotations found in other cultures. Being assertive reflects the ill character of an individual and threatens the harmony and cohesion of interpersonal relationships (Bodde, 1953; Tseng, 1973).

A compliant style of speaking may not appear to be compatible with honest or truthful communication practices. To Chinese, it can be argued that engaging in face-saving and face-negotiating behavior is considered more important than honest and truthful communication. That is, providing the appropriate information at the appropriate time and context with the appropriate persons is more important than honest and truthful communication. For example, a basic rule honored in Chinese culture is "Honor the hierarchy first, your vision of truth second" (Bond, 1991, p. 83). Consistent with this line of reasoning, most Chinese would sacrifice their personal credibility to save mutual face. Compared with Canadians, Chinese view lying as morally less wrong (McLeod & Carment, 1987).

PROVISIONAL RESPONSES

Provisional responses are characteristic of Chinese talk. Chinese rarely give definitively affirmative or negative answers equivalent to "yes" or "no"; rather, replies are carefully and cautiously worded to attend to the needs of both the speaker and the recipient. This orientation is based on and supports some of the fundamental conceptions of communication in Chinese culture. For example, Chinese perceive the response "Sorry. I can't" as "unsubtle" and offensively "frank" (Wierzbicka, 1996). Instead of saying "no" blatantly to a request, Chinese often use such expressions as *bu fang bian* (不方便; "inconvenient") and *you xie kun nan* (有些困难; "there are some difficulties"). These rhetorical responses, as Link (1992) suggests, not only show concern for the face of the petitioner but also save oneself from losing face in the event of rejection from the upper level. To Chinese, concern for face presents little freedom of saying "no" to a request (Wierzbicka, 1996); face saving, sometimes even at the cost of precision, accuracy, and clarity, is the ultimate goal of inter-personal communication.

The ambivalence cast in Chinese responses is also congruent with the cultural belief of *liu you yu di* (留有余地; "making allowances for unforeseen circumstances"). When a "yes" is expressed as *wen ti bu da* (问题不大; "no big problem"), there is room left for retreat. An informant in Young's (1994) study stated aptly, "You need to feel your way and test your boss's mood. If you suspect any negative feedback, you can retreat. Westerners can tolerate failures, but Chinese are traditionally trained in terms of saving face" (p. 163). Furthermore, "Chinese seem to prefer to steadily unravel and build up information before arriving at the important messages" (p. 31). For example, Chinese have the tendency to present all possible conditions to establish the cause and this "because . . . so . . ." pattern of speech can cause problems for others (Young, 1994). In everyday Chinese discourse, expressions such as *yan jiu yan jiu* (研究研究; "We'll study it") and *kao lu kao lu* (考虑考虑; "We'll consider it") suggest that Chinese communication is inherently negotiable. Compromise, intervention, and mediation are an integral part of Chinese communication processes.

USING INTERMEDIARIES

The importance of face further accounts for the use of the intermediary in conflict situations. In general, Chinese are inclined not to confront issues, but when they must, they often rely on others for solutions (Sun, 1994). Through mediation by a third party, Chinese can avoid direct confrontations, which often cause face damage and disruption of interpersonal harmony to the conflicting parties. Many instances of this orientation exist in Chinese culture. It is not unusual, for example, for Chinese to ask a friend to approach a problematic situation and resolve the issue on their behalf. Using a *mei ren* (媒人; "matchmaker") to negotiate with the future in-laws regarding wedding plans is widely practiced out of concern for face saving in the midst of heated arguments and unpleasant disputes (Felty & McDowell, 1994). Ting-Toomey et al. (1991) indicate that Chinese prefer to use a nonconfrontational style of management in face-to-face negotiations.

The role of an intermediary is to protect and save the face of both parties involved in an interpersonal conflict. Given such designated function, an intermediary is often called a "go-between," "mediator," or "peacemaker" (Ma, 1992). Often, an intermediary is known to both parties to ensure fairness and neutrality. Impartiality and face maintenance for both parties in a conflict are the two key factors in any successful mediation (Gabrenya & Hwang, 1996; Ma, 1992). Close friends of both parties and elderly persons respected by both can be unofficial mediators (Ma, 1992) so as to exercise influence on the disputants. Chinese language specialists on a foreign negotiating team are often considered as middle persons between the two teams by Chinese (Pye, 1982). In traditional marriages, *mei ren* often assume the role of go-between and are responsible for mediation in a conflict situation.

YI LUN 议论

The Chinese term *yi lun* means "to gossip" or "to make remarks behind one's back." In Chinese culture, public conversations tend to be ritualized to avoid face-threatening situations. Private conversations, in contrast, tend to be substantive. Consistent with this reasoning is Bond and Lee's (1981) finding that more critical comments are given about a speaker in the speaker-uninformed condition (i.e., the speaker will not hear the comments) than in the audience-informed condition (i.e., the audience will hear the comments). This discrepancy is explained by a Chinese person's concern for the other person's face. In a public conversation, individual views and opinions must yield to the protection of face and the observance of status differences (Bond & Lee, 1981; Yu & Gu, 1990). One way to compensate for this circumspect type of public conversation is to engage in *yi lun*. Yu and Gu (1990) contend that during *yi lun*, Chinese can complain about superiors, parents, teachers, and others who are perceived to have control over them. Chinese utilize the forum of *yi lun* to satisfy their curiosity about others' private lives and the need to speak their true feelings.

The act of *yi lun* not only facilitates expressions of true feelings but also influences how one should behave and relate to others (Bond, 1991). The likelihood of being a target of *yi lun* often decreases when one acts appropriately and makes peace with others. *Yi lun* provides a forum for public exposure and discussion of private information and, when exercised as a lever in personal and social control, often forces the receiver to take some action. *Yi lun* also brings one's face to light for judgment and scrutiny. To Chinese, concern for one's face makes a person vulnerable not only to what others have said but also to the anticipation of potential gossip. Yu (1990) argues that the concern for what others would say usually creates unbearable pressure on Chinese. The fear of being criticized and ridiculed by others has a controlling effect on Chinese behavior. For example, Chinese are reluctant to reveal negative emotions (Cody, Lee, & Chao, 1989; O'Hair, Cody, Wang, & Chao, 1990). Kleinman and Good (1985) suggest that Chinese conceal "dysphoria" (depression, sadness, and irritability) because it brings shame to the self and the family.

The communicative consequence of *yi lun* can be linked to the role of self-disclosure in Chinese personal relationships. Given that private information can be a potential topic for *yi lun,* the fear of losing face in public makes one reluctant to expose intimate information to others. Therefore, personal disclosure of face-threatening information is limited to those with whom trust has been established and proven. Chinese students in junior high schools, for example, prefer to self-disclose to their mothers, followed by their best friends, fathers, and ordinary friends, with regard to topics of general affairs and family. On topics related to sex, their best friends are the preferred target (Yang & Hwang, 1980). This pattern is very different from that in other cultures. For example, North Americans tend to use self-disclosure as a relational strategy to initiate personal relationships. The amount or level of self-disclosure is a part of the relationship development process. It is not uncommon for a Chinese to know more about a North American classmate's personal life than that of a close Chinese friend.

◆ Conclusion

In this chapter, we examined the concept of *mian zi,* discussed the implications of the concern for *mian zi* in Chinese culture, and explicated face-directed communication strategies. As an enduring social and personal concern, *mian zi* influences how Chinese perceive themselves, relate to others, and communicate with others. The skillful employment of communication strategies, such as nonconfrontation, compliance strategies, provisional responses, using intermediaries, and *yi lun,* is essential to effective facework management in Chinese culture.

5

Miscommunication Between Chinese and North Americans

Chinese adages
Pang qiao ce ji (旁敲侧击; "Beat around the bush")
Yi zai yan wai (意在言外; "Meaning lies beyond words")

North American adages
Don't beat around the bush
Say what you mean

In previous chapters, we examined Chinese communication characteristics and underlying cultural premises and philosophies. Compared with Chinese, North Americans comply with an entirely different set of norms and rules of social interaction. When Chinese and North Americans abiding by two distinctive cultural scripts attempt to communicate, miscommunication often follows. In this chapter, we highlight several areas in which Chinese and North Americans clash in their everyday interactions. We discuss specific domains of Chinese-North American communication divergence and conclude with recommendations for ways to improve that communication.

◆ Chinese-North American Communication in a Dilemma

The following two exchange episodes, which we reconstructed from numerous incidents of Chinese-North American miscommunication, demonstrate continuous misunderstanding, confusion, and disarray present in Chinese-North American interactions:

1. *Chinese:*   I just know you don't like my idea.
   American: How? I didn't say a word.
2. *American:* You said yes.
   Chinese: That doesn't mean I agree.

These interaction scenes represent typical instances of how Chinese and North Americans (mis)read one another in their daily encounters. The episodes further illustrate that a simple message can be misconstrued, misinterpreted, and misunderstood when conflicting cultural scripts are put to use. Cultural differences inevitably create barriers to effective intercultural communication.

Chinese and North Americans operate on different sets of assumptions, concerns, expectations, and scripts in their communication. Consequently, they speak differently, respond to compliments differently, engage in different forms of polite interaction, adopt different ways of making requests, and so on. In essence, Chinese and North Americans approach communication in very different ways, and thus, their communication can often be difficult and problematic. Descriptions such as *indirect* versus *direct*, *implicit* versus *explicit*, and *unassertive* versus *assertive* represent some of the ways that differentiate Chinese and North American communication.

As discussed in previous chapters, Chinese communication is influenced by Chinese self-conception, Chinese beliefs about talk, Chinese personal relationship development processes, and the concern for *mian zi*. The relational and other-oriented nature of the Chinese self and the importance of maintaining harmonious relationships in Chinese culture permeate all indigenous concepts of Chinese communication. Consequently, Chinese communication is situated in relationships rather than in individual persons, and others' perceptions and views are critical to the interpretation of various messages. *Han xu* (含蓄) or implicit communication, *ting hua* (听话) or listening centeredness, *ke qi* (客气) or politeness, *zi ji ren* (自己人) or a focus on insiders, and *mian zi* (面子) or face-directed communication strategies are five key aspects of Chinese speaking practices. These five aspects create problematic communication between Chinese and North Americans.

In this chapter, we have isolated the following eight areas of communication divergence between Chinese and North Americans based on the five aspects of Chinese speaking practices: (a) the importance of what is not said versus what is said, (b) the use of *we* versus *I*, (c) polite versus impolite talk, (d) indirect versus direct talk, (e) hesitant versus assertive speech, (f) self-effacing versus self-enhancing talk, (g) private versus public personal questions, and (h) reticent versus expressive speech. These differences appear to create most difficulties for both Chinese and North Americans, and they serve to contextualize the five key characteristics of Chinese speaking practices.

◆ What Is Not Said Versus What Is Said

In Chinese culture, words are not accorded with the same degree of significance found in the U.S. culture. Chinese tend not to take words literally; rather, they believe in *yi zai yan wai* (意在言外; "Meaning lies beyond words") and *yi zai bu yan zhong* (意在不言中; "Meaning lies in the unspoken"). In essence, what is not said is often more meaningful and significant than what is said. In conversational exchanges, one is thus required to make inferences, read between the lines, and draw connections through *ti hui* (体会; "to apprehend or to experience") and *zuo mo* (琢磨; "to contemplate or to ponder"). The ability to *ti hui* and *zuo mo* is highly emphasized and essential to accurate interpretations of messages in Chinese culture. Accordingly, for a Chinese, meaning does not stop at words but proceeds as one further engages in comprehension and contemplation. Thus, granting one another an opportunity to *ti hui* and *zuo mo* constitutes an important dimension in the creation of meaning in Chinese communication and supports the other-oriented Chinese self-concept. By being not forthright in expressing oneself, a Chinese leaves room for others to experience and ponder. As a result, direct expressions in Chinese culture tend not to carry the same weight or be as meaningful as those that are indirect.

Furthermore, there is a prevalent belief that words are inadequate to fully articulate the multifaceted and intricate experiences of people as stated in the expression *yan bu jin yi* (言不尽意; "Words are insufficient for complete expression"). Given that words by themselves are incomplete, Chinese assert that what people say may not coincide with what they think or feel. In Chinese culture, people emphasize the fact that some things cannot be expressed by words.

Differences in perceptions of what is said and what is not said unavoidably create a set of predicaments in Chinese-North American communication. For example, Chinese may become frustrated when North Americans take words too literally and insist on an explanation for everything being said. On the contrary, North Americans may be disheartened when Chinese read too much into what is said and leave many things unexplained. The following two episodes of exchange illustrate this divergence:

1. *Chinese:* I'm afraid that our proposal will be turned down.
   American: Why do you say that? Pat said that she likes our proposal.
   Chinese: I have a feeling that she does not really like it. She was just saying that to be nice.
   American: Trust me on this. I know she means it.
   Chinese: Are you sure?
2. *Chinese:* Could you help me with this? I'm taking Chen to pick up his car.
   American: I offered to take him earlier, but he said, "Don't worry. There is no problem."
   Chinese: He was just being polite. He didn't want to impose on you.
   American: I wouldn't mind doing that, but I thought he didn't need a ride.

◆ We Versus I

Another area in which Chinese and North Americans diverge involves how pronouns are utilized in their talk. One's choice of pronouns often evokes different cultural interpretations. Given that Chinese emphasize a "we" identity and an in-group affiliation, and that Chinese selves are embedded in relations with others, Chinese often have a tendency to use the pronoun *we* to express not only group views but also personal ones. Moreover, they are more at ease when speaking as members of a group than as individuals. As Young (1994) explains, Chinese aim to "redirect the communication's authorship to involve others and to efface the speaker's impositional role" (p. 191). Thus, the collective accountability and in-group identification are accentuated in Chinese talk; consequently, precautions need to be taken in differentiating personal views from collective ones.

North Americans, however, stress an "I" identity and individual autonomy as well as accountability. This cultural emphasis is reflected in the pronounced use of *I* in North American talk. Furthermore, North Americans make clear distinctions between personal views and group views in their language. For them, talk primarily serves to affirm personal identity. The North American way of asserting oneself, however, is often perceived as an attempt to draw attention to oneself and as being self-centered, whereas North Americans tend to attribute the Chinese speaking style to a lack of personal opinion, self-assurance, and self-confidence. Consider, for example, the following conversations:

1. *Chinese:* What do you think of the cost reduction plan?

   American: I feel strongly about it. I don't think we should approve the plan because it will bring a lot of harm to our company.

2. *American:* What do you think of the cost reduction plan?

   Chinese: Our company is at a difficult time. We should do our best not to introduce the plan.

◆ Polite Versus Impolite Talk

Chinese newcomers to the United States often ask, "Why do North Americans apologize for everything they have done?" and "Why are North Americans so polite?" North Americans, however, tend to feel that Chinese rarely say "thank you" or "excuse me." Obviously, North Americans and Chinese draw on their own cultural scripts when it comes to polite talk. One notable difference in Chinese-North American communication lies in how and with whom polite expressions, such as "thank you," "please," and "excuse me," are utilized. In the United States, given the heightened concern for individual independence and autonomy, any infringement or imposition, no matter how big or small, requires some form of verbal acknowledgment. Apology and appreciation thus are an integral part of North American everyday talk and used with everyone in every social and relational context, including family members and intimate friends.

The North American rule of politeness, however, does not hold true in Chinese culture. Chinese interactions with strangers or "outsiders" involve little, if any, polite talk, but in established relationships or "insider" interactions, Chinese appear to be quite gracious and polite. Comparatively, overt expressions of apology and gratitude, if used among family members and close friends, are believed to signify formality, detachment, and relational distance rather than informality, attachment, and relational closeness. For example, when a friend was thanked for his helpful information, he responded, "When did you learn to be so polite to me? I hate such politeness, which places me in the position of a stranger" (W. Z. Hu, personal communication, January 2, 1997). Finally, in very close-knit relational networks, feelings of gratitude and apology are expected to be internalized and "intuited." Consequently, a Chinese may interpret the frequent usage of polite terms in a close relationship as a sign of relational distance, whereas a North American may view the absence of such polite terms as being rude and inconsiderate. The following two excerpts of exchange illustrate how Chinese and North Americans apply the rule of politeness very differently:

1. *American wife:*   I'm hungry. Could you please get me some muffins?
   American husband: What kind? The ones we got yesterday?
   American wife: Yes, please.
   American husband: Here you are.
   American wife: Thank you, my dear.
2. *Chinese wife:*   I'm hungry. I want some muffins.
   Chinese husband: What kind? The ones we got yesterday?
   Chinese wife: Yes.
   Chinese husband: Here you are.

◆ Indirect Versus Direct Talk

Graf (1994) observes that "Chinese tend to beat around the bush. They are not forthright enough that Westerners often perceive them as insincere and untrustworthy" (p. 232). Direct versus indirect talk embodies another domain that is indicative of Chinese-North American (mis)communication. As we indicated in Chapter 3, indirectness and directness manifest in many styles and contexts. Here, we focus on a request-making situation and an implicit versus straightforward style. We demonstrate how a simple request such as a ride to the airport can be easily understood among people from the same culture but inevitably misunderstood in an intercultural context. The three episodes of exchange illustrated later are reconstructed by us from real-life situations and a person's inner thoughts are enclosed in parentheses.

In Chinese culture, requests often are implied rather than stated explicitly for the sake of relational harmony and face maintenance. When a hearer detects a request from the conversation with a speaker, the hearer can choose to either grant or deny the request. If the hearer decides to deny a request, he or she usually does not respond to the request or changes the topic of the conversation. The speaker, consequently, discerns the cues from the hearer and drops the request in later conversations. An implicit understanding often exists between a speaker and a hearer in Chinese culture, and it is essential to the maintenance of harmonious interpersonal relationships. For example, consider the following episode of exchange between two Chinese persons:

1. *Chinese 1:* We're going to New Orleans this weekend.
   Chinese 2: How fun! We wish we were going with you. How long are you going to be there?
   Chinese 1: Three days. (I hope she'll offer me a ride to the airport.)
   Chinese 2: (She may want me to give her a ride.) Do you need a ride to the airport? I'll take you.
   Chinese 1: Are you sure it's not too much trouble.
   Chinese 2: It's no trouble at all.
   Chinese 1: Thank you.
   Chinese 2: Don't mention it.

In the United States, requests often are stated directly and clearly. If a person makes a request, he or she is expected to be as direct as possible. Meanwhile, a person has the liberty to decline a request that is put forth. For North Americans, an explicit understanding between a speaker and a hearer is much desired. The following is an example of a conversation between two North Americans:

2. *American 1:* We're going to New Orleans this weekend.
   American 2: How fun! We wish we were going with you. How long are you going to be there? (If she wants a ride, she will ask.)
   American 1: Three days. By the way, we may need a ride to the airport. You think you can take us?
   American 2: Sure. What time?
   American 1: 10:30 p.m. this coming Saturday.

Note that when interlocutors share the same cultural scripts, their communication is most likely to be smooth and effective as exemplified in both the first and second episodes. Misunderstanding, nevertheless, becomes inevitable when Chinese and North Americans, each adhering to a different set of cultural scripts, interact mindlessly. In Episode 3, the Chinese expects the North American counterpart to be able to detect the request implied and offer a ride, whereas the North American awaits a "loud and clear" request from the Chinese partner. Differences of expectations have to do with North Americans' assumption that if one needs help, one will ask for it. Moreover, as Wallach and Metcalf (1995) contend, "To an American, to offer help when it is not wanted is to treat a person like a child or as an incompetent worker [person]" (p. 61). North Americans believe in the need for individual autonomy, whereas Chinese hold that a direct request often poses an undesirable imposition, which is damaging to the harmonious human relationship. Episode 3 illustrates this point:

3. *Chinese:* We're going to New Orleans this weekend.
   American: How fun! We wish we were going with you. How long are you going to be there?
   Chinese: Three days. (I hope she'll offer me a ride to the airport.)
   American: (If she wants a ride, she will ask me.) Have a great time.
   Chinese: (If she wanted to give me a ride, she would have offered. I'd better ask somebody else.) Thanks. I'll see you when I get back.

◆ Hesitant Versus Assertive Speech

To help the Asian staff become self-assured, confident, and forceful in their speech, North American managers set up assertiveness training workshops for them (Wallach & Metcalf, 1995). To North Americans, the ability to speak firmly and openly is a very desirable cultural trait. Assertiveness thus is a sign of strength, and often, an assertive person is perceived as superior, decisive, and resourceful. North American assertive speech, however, is subjected to a different interpretation in Chinese culture. To Chinese, definitive responses, such as "It's good" and "I don't like it," are marks of arrogance and presumption as well as of complacency and inconsideration. Consequently, in personal and social relationships, Chinese rarely give assertive responses and hence appear hesitant to others. Young (1994) indicates that Chinese subordinates tend to use "hedging or softening devices to neutralize assertive nuances" (p. 158). For example, a subordinate was observed to use "somewhat" and "a little better" instead of "good" and "can or cannot" instead of "can" in a conversation with a superior (Young, 1994). Interestingly, Chinese comply with this practice in other aspects of their lives as well. The following are examples of exchange that mark the divergence between Chinese and North Americans:

1. *Chinese:*   Do you like this type of music?
   American: No, I don't care for it at all. To me it's all noise.
2. *American:* Do you like this type of music?
   Chinese: It's a little bit noisy. Otherwise, it's okay.

Furthermore, in Chinese speech, the word *no* is not only restrained but avoided at all costs. Murray (1983) observes that Chinese frequently use *perhaps* and *maybe* to communicate rejections, refusals, and denials. In business negotiations, the word *possible* was shown to denote *no* (Pye, 1992). To a Chinese, when something is suggested as "inconvenient," it means it is impossible. *Wen ti bu ta* (问题不大; "No big problem"), *yan jiu yan jiu* (研究研究; "We'll study it"), or *kao lu kao lu* (考虑考虑; "We'll consider it") are examples of other ways of saying no in Chinese culture. The word *yes* is equally vague and uncertain in Chinese talk. To save face, Chinese may say yes to communicate disagreement. On the other hand, Chinese may say yes to convey that they are listening (Wallach & Metcalf, 1995). Therefore, learning to talk in a hesitant manner and to decipher hidden messages is both desirable and necessary for Chinese.

◆ Self-Effacing Versus Self-Enhancing Talk

Culture also defines how we talk about ourselves. Whereas Chinese cherish self-effacement, humility, and modesty in their talk, North Americans, comparatively speaking, prize the need for verbal self-enhancement, self-affirmation, and self-approval. To Chinese, self-effacing talk is a sign of strength, respectability, and integrity. Thus, they often understate their abilities and accomplishments and become uncomfortable in talking about their achievements. Nevertheless, to North Americans, modesty entails a very different meaning; it implies weakness, incompetence, and a lack of self-confidence. North Americans not only feel it is appropriate to talk about their accomplishments but also believe that they are in the best position to present themselves in a positive light (Wallach & Metcalf, 1995). The following excerpts of conversation from a well-known Chinese TV series provide an excellent illustration of the previously mentioned difference between Chinese and North Americans (Zheng, Zheng, & Feng, 1993):

> Mr. Wang, a native of Beijing, recently came to New York City and is now the boss of a clothing company. Ah Chun, a native of Taiwan educated in the United States, has been a New York City resident for many years. Ah Chun is Mr. Wang's girlfriend.
> [First day of a new company; in the workshop talking to new employees]

> *Wang:*   Hello, everyone. You've been working very hard. Today is the first day of the opening of this company. Each one of you is an expert here. However, I'm only a new hand, so I'm asking you to help me in anyway you can. Thank you very much. . . .

> [Ah Chun interrupting Wang]

> *Ah Chun:*   Mr. Wang is too polite. He is not, as he said, a new hand. Rather, his designs and samples have won big prizes in places like New York and Paris.

> [Now back in the office]

> *Wang:*   [Annoyed] Why don't you be the boss? You can have my job.
> *Ah Chun:*   Well, if you want to be modest, you shouldn't be the boss.
> *Wang:*   There's no need to brag just because you're the boss. I can't believe that you even thought of the New York and Paris stuff.
> *Ah Chun:*   In the U.S., this is called establishing your credentials.

	It's not bragging. Let me tell you when I first came to the U.S., I also was modest. But, I learned if you don't believe in yourself, who will believe in you?
Wang:	What I meant is that you cannot get too far away from the facts. When people find out later on, you get laughed at.
Ah Chun:	Look, I'll tell you something. Here in the U.S., people only recognize one thing: success or failure.

The two modes of talk (self-enhancing and self-effacing) can also be most susceptible to misinterpretations in job interviews and performance evaluations. Given that, in Chinese culture, accomplishments and qualifications are to be recognized and spoken by others, one rarely uses such occasions to promote oneself. A Chinese American explains (Himmel, 1996), "If you're sure of what you are, then you don't need to go telling people what they should think about you" (p. 18). In contrast, North Americans are expected to make a case for themselves to be appreciated and rewarded. As Storti (1994) observes, "Americans see an interview as an exercise of persuasion" (p. 122). To present oneself in a good light is beneficial to one's professional development, and thus, self-enhancing talk is an accepted practice. The following is an extract that typifies many interviews between Chinese and North Americans:

Ms. Jones:	Well, I can see you have a lot of experience in this area. You've been doing this for the past 15 years.
Ms. Wang:	I have some experience.
Ms. Jones:	I understand that your position is very important.
Ms. Wang:	Essentially, everyone is responsible for a particular area, so every position is important.
Ms. Jones:	Ms. Wang, could you tell me what your contribution would be if you join us?
Ms. Wang:	I'll do my best and work hard.

As you can see, the fact that Ms. Wang insisted on downplaying her experience and importance in the company that she worked for can indeed help create a negative image of her in the mind of the North American interviewer. The opposite effect, however, occurs if the interviewer is Chinese. Wallach and Metcalf (1995) note that North Americans are perceived by Asians as inappropriately boastful, whereas Asians are regarded by North Americans as inappropriately modest. They suggest that Asians working with North Americans should share their achievements and accomplishments at annual job evaluations and performance reviews even though it may be uncomfortable and difficult for them. That is, to be recognized and rewarded, Asians in the United States need to engage in self-enhancing talk.

◆ Private Versus Public Personal Questions

Another area of predicament in Chinese-North American communication involves differences in the domain and the meaning of private and public personal questions. In Chinese conversations, questions concerning age, marital status, past experiences, occupation, income, and place of residence belong to the public domain and are solicited routinely by interlocutors (Hu & Grove, 1991; Jing, 1991). Chinese do not perceive these questions as impingements on personal privacy but rather as ways of establishing relationships and showing concern. Elder persons, for example, may inquire of younger persons about their marital status and the number of their children in their initial conversation to demonstrate interest and care.

Thus, *guan xing* (关心; "to show concern") talk is a communicative genre that occupies a prominent position in Chinese relational communication. *Guan xing* entails asking questions about a person's well-being and other personal matters. One of the most frequently asked questions that demonstrate *guan xing*, for example, is, "How is your health situation lately?" (Jing, 1991). "To show concern" also evokes the use of cautionary remarks, such as "You should not drink too much because it is not good for your health" or "You should put on some warm clothes because it is cold outside," in interpersonal interactions. *Quan jie* (劝解; "to caution and to advise") is widely employed to show concern for others in Chinese culture (Jing, 1991).

North Americans, however, do not appreciate others asking questions about their financial situation, age, family status, or appearance (Wallach & Metcalf, 1995). They consider them as highly private personal questions. Even though Chinese may ask these questions with the best intentions, North Americans tend to interpret them as an intrusion to their privacy and individual freedom (Jing, 1991; Lin, 1993). To many North Americans who value individuality and independence over group harmony and interdependence, the discourse of *guan xing* can be misconstrued as disturbingly patronizing, condescending, and offensive. The following conversation provides a clear illustration of the Chinese-North American divergence in this respect:

American 1:	Good to see you back. How was Beijing?
American 2:	Wonderful! I had lots of good food and the weather was not bad at all.
American 1:	I'd love to go there sometime.
American 2:	Those Chinese, you know, they really took good care of you. I felt as though I were being mothered the entire time I was there. They kept telling me what to do and what not to do. You know, it can be overbearing sometimes, but I guess they had good intentions.
American 1:	I was told that Chinese don't like to leave their guests alone. Is that true?

◆ Reticent Versus Expressive Speech

Chinese and North Americans often are not in sync with one another when it comes to speaking in public. North Americans usually enjoy the act of speaking and assume the role of the speaker, whereas Chinese willingly accept the role of the attentive listener. To Chinese, it seems that speaking comes naturally to North Americans because they are verbally articulate and talkative. To North Americans, however, Chinese are naturally shy. Speaking in public or in front of strangers appears to be a stressful event for many Chinese.

These perceptions, to a great extent, stem from the daily practices of different speaking and listening styles in these two cultures. In the United States, for example, a strong emphasis on verbal communication skills can be found at home, in school, and at work. Parents stress the need for verbal and assertive expression of their children, teachers encourage students to participate in class discussions and to present their ideas verbally, and employees are expected to verbalize their ideas and views in meetings and to give oral presentations. Persuasive speaking is a powerful vehicle and a way of life in the United States. To North Americans, talk can affirm self-identity, boost self-confidence, generate ideas, explicate thoughts and beliefs, convey personal opinions, express feelings, and solve problems. Most North Americans believe that if one has a problem with someone, the two people should talk it through.

In contrast, verbal communication skills are not emphasized at home, in school, or at work in Chinese culture. The uneasiness that Chinese often experience in public speaking not only is due to a lack of training and practice in the area but also is a result of heightened concern for relational outcomes. Harmony, unity, and hierarchy are important considerations for Chinese, but they often are at risk when divergent views, opinions, and ideas are discussed openly. Therefore, speaking can pose an immediate threat to various relational qualities such as *mian zi* ("face"), *guan xi* ("connections"), status, and *gan qing* ("feelings"). For example, when one seeks to express disagreement openly, one inevitably risks losing face and endangering personal relationships. Words, if not properly and cautiously used, have the potential of hurting others' feelings. In Chinese culture, speaking spectacles, such as debate and argumentation, are desirable only in the intellectual arena. Given the relational focus of speaking in Chinese culture, Chinese often are reminded to be discreet in their everyday speech.

◆ Improving Chinese-North American Communication

Comparable to communication with unfamiliar others in one's own culture, effective and satisfactory Chinese-North American communication begins with and depends on shared knowledge and bilateral understanding. One's knowledge and understanding, however, should not merely end with dos and don'ts in a particular culture because each interaction, whether intracultural or intercultural, is unique to a specific situation and the parties involved. A prescriptive approach such as saying "yes" here and "no" there does not warrant much utility in improving Chinese-North American communication. One needs to understand not only different aspects of communication divergence but also why the divergence exists. By looking at the deeper cultural structures and premises that underlie the communication processes, one can accurately diagnose and analyze various communicative acts and respond to each situation appropriately and competently. Consequently, much of this book is devoted to understanding the underlying cultural assumptions and expectations of Chinese communication practices.

Furthermore, improving Chinese-North American communication requires a mind-set that is open, sensitive, responsive, and adaptive, as well as an ability to modify or restrain one's own cultural way of speaking. Developing skills such as being perceptive, asking questions, and negotiating meanings is also conducive to effective Chinese-North American communication. Through trial and error, patient observation, and adaptive practices, one learns what is acceptable and appropriate in one culture but not in another culture.

In addition to the general principles stated previously, attention must be given to the specific areas of cultural differences between Chinese and North Americans and their impact on everyday speaking practices. In improving communication with Chinese, North Americans must be aware that the Chinese self is other oriented and relational in nature. Chinese self-development is connected closely with the self's orientation to others' needs, wishes, and expectations. Developing and maintaining relationships, especially harmonious relationships, being aware of one's position in relation to others, and acting one's role appropriately are crucial to the recognition, definition, and completion of the self. This unique focus of Chinese self-construal thus creates a communication pattern that is situated in relationships rather than in individual persons, aims to preserve harmonious relations with others, and places a value on implicit communication, listening, polite talk, insider-outsider differentiation, and face-saving strategies. To help North Americans better communicate with Chinese, we present the following list of guidelines that represent the key aspects of the Chinese way of speaking discussed in this book:

1. Focus on how something is said—relational and mutual-face meanings often outweigh literal, content meanings.
2. Learn to read paralinguistic cues, such as facial expressions, body movements, gestures, and pauses.
3. Develop a belief that words can be inadequate and insufficient.
4. Understand that Chinese selves are often embedded in plural pronouns, and learn to differentiate personal opinions from those of the group.
5. Be aware that impersonal language can be used with outsiders and that insiders and outsiders are treated differently.
6. Accept that Chinese value indirect talk and that requests are often implied.
7. Recognize that definitive responses are rarely given in Chinese culture and that the word *yes* may have multiple meanings.
8. Understand that modesty is a Chinese virtue and that understating and discrediting oneself is expected.
9. Be aware that personal questions considered as private in the United States are asked frequently and that *guan xing* talk is a sign of care and interest.
10. Accept that Chinese tend to keep opinions to themselves and are uncomfortable in engaging in social talk with strangers.

Chinese, however, need to understand that the self in the United States is independent and complete. To North Americans, relationships with others are based on equality and respect for autonomy and privacy. The notion of "other" does not assume the same level of importance as found in Chinese culture. Communication in the United States is thus self-oriented and used primarily to affirm self-identity and to achieve individual needs and goals. Given this unique focus of the self in the United States, North Americans tend to value direct communication, the ability to speak, assertiveness, and being an individual. In helping Chinese improve their communication with North Americans, we provide the following recommendations derived from the previous discussion in this chapter:

1. Focus on what is said; try not to read too much into the words or be oversensitive to nonverbal nuances.
2. Learn to accept what is said.
3. Develop a belief that verbal messages and feedback are powerful and effective.
4. Understand that self-affirmation and individuality are important to North Americans and that self-oriented messages are used to separate oneself from others.
5. Be aware that everyone should be treated equally and that polite speech applies to family members, intimate friends, and strangers.
6. Accept that North Americans value direct talk and that requests are often stated explicitly.
7. Recognize that being assertive is valued in the U.S. culture and that "no" is accepted as an assertive response.
8. Understand that modesty is equated with low self-confidence and that enhancing and crediting oneself is expected.
9. Learn not to ask personal questions, because they can be offensive and insulting; understand that *guan xing* talk may be construed as meddling and intrusive.
10. Accept that North Americans like to express their opinions openly and are talkative in their social interactions.

Epilogue

In this book, we have identified, described, and conceptualized some of the distinctive communication practices in Chinese culture from the self-OTHER perspective. One of our objectives in writing this book was to make a concerted effort to "make explicit what is implicit." We hope this book will serve as a useful stepping-stone toward advancing your understanding of Chinese communication and its situated cultural context. Given the lack of systematic research in Chinese communication patterns, we were unable to address many issues in an in-depth manner. Much future work, therefore, is needed to provide a theoretical, empirical, and contextualized account of the way of communicating in Chinese culture. Here, we will first address some of the conceptual and methodological limitations of our current discussion and then present several fruitful areas for conducting communication research in the future.

◆ Limitations

Given that there is a limited amount of theorizing and research in Chinese communication practices, we were only able to present some working knowledge concerning this area. Our conceptions, interpretations, analyses, and conclusions are based primarily on the newly developed model, the self-OTHER perspective. Needless to say, many of the theoretical observations must be tested and

87

verified empirically in future studies. Furthermore, our discussion of Chinese communication practices is neither exclusive nor exhaustive. Many other communication practices await further investigation. One such practice, for example, is *guan xing* (关心; "to show concern"). *Guan xing* is an everyday vocabulary that the vast majority of Chinese use in their interpersonal encounters. *Guan xing* talk embodies the relational focus of Chinese communication and is widely used to initiate and consolidate personal relationships. Therefore, it is necessary for us to pay close attention to vocabularies and metaphors that Chinese utilize in their daily lives to achieve a deeper level of understanding of Chinese communication practices.

In addition, research findings included in this book primarily are from survey-based studies. Self-report data not only are confined to the preestablished scope of the inquiry but also are limited to perceptions of actual communication practices. Chinese communication research needs to examine actual communicative behaviors in addition to thoughts (Ma, 1990). Research on Chinese communication, therefore, will benefit tremendously from studies of actual discourse taking place in naturalistic settings, open-ended in-depth interviews, and ethnographic observations (Hymes, 1974). Rich descriptions gained from those methods will help better conceptualize and understand Chinese communication practices. The use of cultural scripts formulated according to lexical universals also lends itself to analyzing and explaining communication patterns (Wierzbicka, 1996). Wierzbicka's approach of cultural scripts seems to be much more revealing in explicating culture-specific norms and ways of communicating than are binary labels such as *direct* and *indirect*. Finally, the study of communication practices in an experimental setting provides yet another useful alternative. Exploring how Chinese actually respond to a particular structured situation has generated some provocative findings (Bond & Venus, 1991; Pierson & Bond, 1982). Understanding of communication similarities and differences can be further refined by comparing Chinese experimental interactions with those of other cultural groups.

example of a behavioral rule is the "face concern" rule, which declares that if a conflict arises, the best strategy is to avoid it (Liu, 1986). In addition to identifying behavioral rules, the cultural level of investigation entails seeking out emic concepts that significantly define everyday Chinese communication practices. An example of one such concept is *mian zi* (面子). As Young (1994) asserts, "Face [*mian zi*] goes deep to the core of a Chinese person's identity and integrity" (p. 19). "*Mian zi* talk" makes up a unique genre of Chinese communication, and it has a profound impact on Chinese daily personal and social interactions. It thus warrants further exploration and observation. Another Chinese genre of talk involves the notions of *zi ji ren* (自己人; "insiders") and *wai ren* (外人; "outsiders"). Careful and close examinations of questions such as how Chinese talk to insiders (i.e., "insider talk") compared with outsiders (i.e., "outsider talk") will contribute to our further understanding of characteristics of Chinese communication.

Furthermore, the cultural level of analysis can focus on identifying what types of speech acts or tasks are most likely to create cultural misinterpretations and misunderstanding. One way to accomplish this is to examine how various speech acts or tasks have been conceptually defined by Chinese observers and to pinpoint the relational properties or dimensions they possess. An investigation of culture-specific meanings of various speech acts or tasks will help us understand and better interpret existing cross-cultural differences and overlaps. For example, unlike North Americans, Chinese distinguish disagreement from injury and disappointment, and they also exhibit a lower level of discontent with disagreement than with injury and disappointment (Ma, 1990). This finding can be attributed to the fact that disagreement, injury, and disappointment are viewed differently in two cultures. We presume that Chinese would view disagreement as less face threatening to personal relationships than injury or disappointment because disagreement is more task related in the Chinese interaction context than are injury or disappointment. North Americans, however, are likely to conceptualize them as situations in which the independent self has been challenged, and a response is warranted. They tend not to perceive that one message can possess multiple layers of face implications. Another approach entails conducting in-depth analyses of speech acts such as giving explanation, arguing over a point, taking a position on a controversial issue, making requests, asking for favors, giving compliments, making excuses, refusing, dealing with conflicts, negotiating contracts, and expressing personal opinions. To uncover cultural expectations and assumptions embedded in these speech acts will help improve communication between Chinese and others.

The second level of inquiry (i.e., social level of inquiry) provides another fertile area for future research. Our understanding of Chinese communication processes will be broadened and deepened when variables such as gender, age, education, social status, regional dialect, and geographical or regional location are taken into consideration. Gilligan (1993) argues that "since masculinity is defined through separation while femininity is defined through attachment, male gender identity is threatened by intimacy while female gender identity is threatened by separation" (p. 8). The contrastive needs of men and women in their developmental processes thus give rise to gendered communication practices. Imperative questions that need to be addressed include the following: To what extent is Gilligan's assessment applicable to Chinese culture? How do we characterize Chinese women's communication practices compared with those of Chinese men? Is *mian zi*, for example, a more or less significant concern for Chinese women than for Chinese men? Age is another variable that needs to be examined in connection with Chinese communication practices. Younger people and older people construct their social realities differently. For example, older Chinese people (50+ years) assign greater importance to harmonious family relations and contributions to society, whereas younger Chinese people (29-49 years) view true love, living happily, and enjoying life as more important (Chu & Ju, 1993). Regional disparity in children's socialization can also be attributed to differences in communication within the Chinese cultural milieu. In one study, an overwhelming majority of parents in Shanghai and a slight majority of parents in Singapore endorsed the statement, "Parents should not display intimacy in the presence of their child," but parents in Taiwan did not endorse the statement and indicated that it is not improper for parents to show intimacy in front of their child. Moreover, Chinese parents in Taiwan do not think that children should be assertive, whereas those in Singapore permit their children to be assertive (Wu, 1996). Within China, dialect variations in different regions can also create a profound effect on the content and the intensity of the different types of relational talk.

The third level of analysis, the communication level, focuses on various dimensions of specific communicative acts and their implications for everyday speaking practices. To fully understand how Chinese give and receive compliments, for example, we first need to examine the domain of compliments. That is, what are appropriate "complimenting zones" (e.g., personal appearance, achievement, and luck) in Chinese culture? We then need to determine in what situations Chinese are expected to receive compliments and in what situations they are to reject them in a self-effacing manner. Identifying skillful versus unskillful complimenting interaction strategies is yet another important part of this research process. This multidimensional approach to the study of communication has helped generate some illuminating results that led us to rethink, redefine, and redesign the scope of our investigation. One such example involves the study of assertiveness (Chan, 1993). Moving away from viewing assertiveness as a unidimensional construct, Chan argues that assertiveness is a multidimensional construct and situation specific. His study of Hong Kong students reveals that assertive responses are achievement related and unassertive responses are expressions of negative feelings, needs, and dissatisfaction, thus providing support for his argument (Chan, 1993).

◆ Conclusion

In this book, we have examined the Chinese self-construal, Chinese personal relationship development processes, Chinese speaking practices, the concept of *mian zi,* and problematic areas of communication between Chinese and North Americans. Our analysis of Chinese communication is situated in a discussion and an investigation of the Chinese cultural context. We believe that without a sound understanding of Chinese cultural premises and assumptions concerning communication, full comprehension of why Chinese communicate the way they do and how to actually engage in effective communication with them will not be possible. Thus, the purpose of this book is to provide both a conceptual and a practical guide to understanding communication practices in Chinese culture. We hope this book is successful in addressing some of the issues that have concerned many about Chinese communication patterns. Finally, we envision that this book will not only spark interest in the study of Chinese communication practices but also, more important, help raise some challenging questions for future theory development and research in this area.

References

Argyle, M., Henderson, M., Bond, M. H., Iizuka, Y., & Contarello, A. (1986). Cross-cultural variations in relationship rules. *International Journal of Psychology, 21,* 287-315.

Barnett, A. D. (1979). The communication system in China: Some generalizations, hypotheses, and questions for research. In G. C. Chu & F. L. K. Hsu (Eds.), *Moving a mountain: Cultural changes in China* (pp. 386-395). Honolulu: University Press of Hawaii.

Bi, X. (1994). Zhong guo ren de xiang shui [Chinese perfume]. In Y. Bo (Ed.), *Zhong guo ren, ni shou le shen me zhu zhou?* (pp. 67-73). Taipei, Taiwan: Xing guang chu ban she.

Bo, Y. (1992). *The ugly Chinaman and the crisis of Chinese culture* (D. J. Cohn & J. Qing, Eds. & Trans.). Sydney, Australia: Allen & Unwin.

Bodde, D. (1953). Harmony and conflict in Chinese philosophy. In A. F. Wright (Ed.), *Studies in Chinese thought* (pp. 19-80). Chicago: University of Chicago Press.

Bond, M. H. (1991). *Beyond the Chinese face.* Hong Kong: Oxford University Press.

Bond, M. H. (1993). Emotions and their expression in Chinese culture. *Journal of Nonverbal Behavior, 17,* 245-262.

Bond, M. H., & Hwang, K. K. (1986). The social psychology of Chinese people. In M. H. Bond (Ed.), *The psychology of the Chinese people* (pp. 213-266). Oxford, UK: Oxford University Press.

Bond, M., & Lee, P. (1981). Face saving in Chinese culture: A discussion and experimental study of Hong Kong students. In A. Y. C. King & R. P. L. Lee (Eds.), *Social life and development in Hong Kong* (pp. 289-304). Hong Kong: Chinese University Press.

Bond, M. H., Leung, K., & Wan, K. C. (1982). The social impact of self-effacing attributions: The Chinese case. *Journal of Social Psychology, 118,* 157-166.

Bond, M. H., & Venus, C. K. (1991). Resistance to group or personal insults in an ingroup or outgroup context. *International Journal of Psychology, 26,* 83-94.

Brown, P., & Levinson, S. (1987). *Politeness: Some universals in language usage.* Cambridge, UK: Cambridge University Press.

Chan, D. W. (1993). Components of assertiveness: Their relationships with assertive rights and depressed mood among Chinese college students in Hong Kong. *Behavior Research and Therapy, 31,* 529-538.

Chang, H. C. (1992, May). *The concepts of Pao and human emotional debt in Chinese interpersonal relationships and communication.* Paper presented at the Annual International Communication Association Convention, Miami, FL.

Chang, H. C., & Holt, G. R. (1994). A Chinese perspective on face as inter-relational concern. In S. Ting-Toomey (Ed.), *The challenge of facework* (pp. 95-132). Albany: State University of New York Press.

Chen, F. T. (1991). The Confucian view of world order. *Indiana International and Comparative Law Review, 1,* 45-69.

Cheng, S. K. (1990). Understanding the culture and behavior of East Asians—A Confucian perspective. *Australian and New Zealand Journal of Psychiatry, 24,* 510-515.

Chiang, O. (1989). On face and credibility. *Chinese American Forum, 5*(1), 14.

Chinese Culture Connection. (1987). Chinese values and the search for culture-free dimensions of culture. *Journal of Cross-Cultural Psychology, 18,* 143-164.

Chiu, M. M. (1984). *The Tao of Chinese religion.* New York: University Press of America.

Chu, G. C. (1985). The changing concept of self in contemporary China. In A. J. Marsella, G. DeVos, & F. L. K. Hsu (Eds.), *Culture and self: Asian and Western perspectives* (pp. 252- 277). New York: Tavistock.

Chu, G. C. (1989). Change in China: Where have you gone Mao Zedong? *Centerview* (East-West Center), *3,* 7.

Chu, G. C., & Ju, Y. A. (1993). *The great wall in ruins: Communication and cultural change in China.* Albany: State University of New York Press.

Cody, M. J., Lee, W. S., & Chao, E. Y. (1989). Telling lies: Correlates of deception among Chinese. In J. Forgas & M. Innes (Eds.), *Recent advances in social psychology: An international perspective* (pp. 359-368). Amsterdam: North Holland.

Cupach, W., & Metts, S. (1994). *Facework.* Thousand Oaks, CA: Sage.

DeVos, G., & Abbot, K. A. (1966). *The Chinese family in San Francisco.* Unpublished master's thesis, University of California, Berkeley.

Dien, D. S.-F. (1983). Big me and little me: A Chinese perspective on self. *Psychiatry, 46,* 281-286.

Dion, K. L., & Dion, K. K. (1988). Romantic love: Individual and cultural perspectives. In R. J. Sternberg & M. L. Barnes (Eds.), *The psychology of love* (pp. 264-289). New Haven, CT: Yale University Press.

Fairbank, J. K. (1991). The old order. In R. F. Dernberger, K. J. DeWoskin, J. M. Goldstein, R. Murphey, & M. K. Whyte (Eds.), *The Chinese* (pp. 31-37). Ann Arbor: University of Michigan, Center for Chinese Studies.

Felty, J., & McDowell, B. (1994, May). John's Taiwanese wedding. *United Airlines Hemispheres,* pp. 66-69.

Gabrenya, W. K., & Hwang, K. K. (1996). Chinese social interaction: Harmony and hierarchy on the good earth. In M. H. Bond (Ed.), *The handbook of Chinese psychology* (pp. 309-321). Hong Kong: Oxford University Press.

Gao, G. (1993, May). *A test of the triangular theory of love in Chinese and American romantic relationships.* Paper presented at the Annual International Communication Association Convention, Washington, DC.

Gao, G. (1996). Self and other: A Chinese perspective on interpersonal relationships. In W. B. Gudykunst, S. Ting-Toomey, & T. Nishida (Eds.), *Communication in personal relationships across cultures* (pp. 81-101). Thousand Oaks, CA: Sage.

Gao, G. (in press). An initial analysis of the effects of face and concern for "other" in Chinese interpersonal communication. *International Journal of Intercultural Relations.*

Gao, G., & Gudykunst, W. B. (1995). Attributional confidence, perceived similarity, and network involvement in Chinese and American romantic relationships. *Communication Quarterly, 43,* 431-445.

Gao, G., Ting-Toomey, S., & Gudykunst, W. B. (1996). Chinese communication processes. In M. H. Bond (Ed.), *The handbook of Chinese psychology* (pp. 280-293). Hong Kong: Oxford University Press.

Gilligan, C. (1993). *In a different voice: Psychological theory and women's development.* Cambridge, MA: Harvard University Press.

Goffman, E. (1955). On face-work: An analysis of ritual elements in social interaction. *Journal of the Study of International Processes, 18,* 213-231.

Graf, J. (1994). Zhong guo ren mian mian guan [Views on Chinese]. In Y. Bo (Ed.), *Zhong guo ren, ni shou le shen me zhu zhou?* (pp. 232-234). Taipei, Taiwan: Xing guang chu ban she.

Gu, Y. G. (1990). Politeness phenomena in modern Chinese. *Journal of Pragmatics, 14,* 237-257.

Gu, Y. J. (1990). Nei wai you bie, qi ke bu fen: "Zi ji ren" he "wai ren" de ren ji yun dong [How could you not make a distinction between an insider and an outsider?] In *Zhong guo ren de xing li: Vol. 3. Zhong guo ren de mian ju xing ge: Ren qing yu mian zi* (pp. 28-39). Taipei, Taiwan: Zhang lao shi chu ban she.

Gudykunst, W. B., Gao, G., & Franklyn-Stokes, A. (1996). Self-monitoring and concern for social appropriateness in China and England. In J. Pandey, D. Sinha, & D. P. S. Bhawuk (Eds.), *Asian contributions to cross-cultural psychology* (pp. 255-267). New Delhi, India: Sage.

Gudykunst, W. B., Gao, G., Schmidt, K. L., Nishida, T., Bond, M. H., Leung, K., Wang, G., & Barraclough, R. (1992). The influence of individualism-collectivism on communication in ingroup and outgroup relationships. *Journal of Cross-Cultural Psychology, 23,* 196-213.

Gumperz, J. J. (1994). Foreword. In L. W. L. Young (Ed.), *Crosstalk and culture in Sino-American communication* (pp. xiii-xix). Cambridge, UK: Cambridge University Press.

Hall, E. T. (1976). *Beyond culture.* New York: Doubleday.

Hellweg, S. A., Samovar, L. A., & Skow, L. (1991). Cultural variations in negotiation styles. In L. A. Samovar & R. E. Porter (Eds.), *Intercultural communication: A reader* (6th ed., pp. 66-78). Belmont, CA: Wadsworth.

Hildebrandt, H. W. (1988). A Chinese managerial view of business communication. *Management Communication Quarterly, 2,* 217-234.

Himmel, S. (1996, June 16). The quiet hero. *San Jose Mercury News West,* pp. 16-18.

Ho, D. Y. F. (1976). On the concept of face. *American Journal of Sociology, 81,* 867-884.

Hofstede, G. (1980). *Culture's consequences: International differences in work-related values.* Beverly Hills, CA: Sage.

Hsu, F. L. (1970). *Americans and Chinese.* Garden City, NY: Natural History Press.

Hsu, F. L. (1971). Eros, affect and pao. In F. L. K. Hsu (Ed.), *Kinship and culture* (pp. 439-475). Chicago: Aldine.

Hsu, F. L. (1981). *Americans and Chinese: Passage to difference* (3rd ed.). Honolulu: University Press of Hawaii.

Hsu, L. K. (Producer), & Lee, A. (Director). (1994). *Eat drink man woman* [Film]. Taipei, Taiwan: Central Motion Picture Corporation.

Hu, H. C. (1944). The Chinese concepts of "face." *American Anthropologist, 46,* 45-64.

Hu, W. Z., & Grove, C. L. (1991). *Encountering the Chinese: A guide for Americans.* Yarmouth, ME: Intercultural Press.

Hwang, K. K. (1987). Face and favor: The Chinese power game. *American Journal of Sociology, 92,* 944-974.

Hwang, K. K. (1990). Gui fan xing guan xi he gong ju xing guan xi [Regulative and instrumental relations]. In *Zhong guo ren de xing li: Vol. 8. Zhong guo ren de shi jian you xi: Ren qing yu shi gu* (pp. 57-63). Tapei, Taiwan: Zhang lao shi chu ban she.

Hymes, D. (1974). Ways of speaking. In R. Bauman & J. Shazer (Eds.), *Explorations in the ethnography of speaking* (pp. 433-451). Cambridge, UK: Cambridge University Press.

Jing, Z. K. (1991, June). Ru he xuan ze tong wai guo ren jiao tan de hua ti [How to select topics in conversations with foreigners]. *Yan jiang yu gou cai, 5-6.*

King, A. Y., & Bond, M. H. (1985). The Confucian paradigm of man: A sociological view. In W. S. Tseng & D. H. Wu (Eds.), *Chinese culture and mental health* (pp. 29-45). Orlando, FL: Academic Press.

King, A. Y., & Myers, J. T. (1977). *Shame as an incomplete conception of Chinese culture: A study of face.* Hong Kong: Chinese University of Hong Kong, Social Research Center.

Kleinman, A. (1980). *Patients and healers in the context of culture.* Berkeley: University of California Press.

Kleinman, A., & Good, B. (1985). *Culture and depression: Studies in the anthropology and cross-cultural psychiatry of affect and disorder.* Berkeley: University of California Press.

Krone, K., Garrett, M., & Chen, L. (1992). Managerial communication practices in Chinese factories: A preliminary investigation. *Journal of Business Communication, 29,* 229-252.

Lesser, G. S. (1976). Cultural differences in learning and thinking styles. In S. Messick (Ed.), *Individuality in learning* (pp. 137-160). San Francisco: Jossey-Bass.

Lesser, G. S., Fifer, G., & Clark, D. H. (1965). Mental abilities of children from different social class and cultural groups. *Monograph of the Society for Research in Child Development, 30*(4).

Leung, K. (1988). Some determinants of conflict avoidance. *Journal of Cross-Cultural Psychology, 19,* 125-136.

Li, S.-H. (1986). *You shi jie guan kan xian dai zhong guo ren* [Looking at modern Chinese from a world view]. Taipei, Taiwan: Huang guan chu ban she.

Liang, Q. C. (1936). *Yin Ping Shih Wen Chi* [Collected works of Liang Chi Chao]. Taipei, Taiwan: Culture Books.

Lim, T.-S. (1994). Facework and interpersonal relationships. In S. Ting-Toomey (Ed.), *The challenge of facework: Cross-cultural and interpersonal issues* (pp. 209-229). Albany: State University of New York Press.

Lim, T.-S., & Bowers, J. (1991). Face-work: Solidarity, approbation, and tact. *Human Communication Research, 17,* 415-450.

Lin, C. F. (1993). *Du hui xin nu xing: Vol. 13. Gen lao wai tan lian ai* [Dating with foreigners]. Taipei, Taiwan: SITAK.

Lindsay, C. P., & Dempsey, B. L. (1985). Experiences in training Chinese business people to use U.S. management techniques. *Journal of Applied Behavioral Science, 21,* 65-78.

Link, P. (1992). *Evening chats in Beijing: Probing China's predicament.* New York: Norton.

Littlejohn, S. W. (1992). *Theories of human communication* (4th ed.). Belmont, CA: Wadsworth.

Liu, I.-M. (1986). Chinese cognition. In M. H. Bond (Ed.), *The psychology of the Chinese people* (pp. 73-105). Hong Kong: Oxford University Press.

Ma, R. G. (1990). An exploratory study of discontented responses in American and Chinese relationships. *Southern Communication Journal, 55,* 305-318.

Ma, R. G. (1992). The role of unofficial intermediaries in interpersonal conflicts in the Chinese culture. *Communication Quarterly, 40,* 269-278.

MacCormack, G. (1991). Cultural values in traditional Chinese law. *Chinese Culture, 32*(4), 1-11.

Markus, H. R., & Kitayama, S. (1991). Culture and the self: Implications for cognition, emotion, motivation. *Psychological Review, 98,* 224-253.

McLeod, B. A., & Carment, D. W. (1987). *To lie or not to lie: A comparison of Canadian and Chinese attitudes towards deception.* Unpublished manuscript, McMaster University, Hamilton, Ontario, Canada.

Murray, D. P. (1983). Face to face: American and Chinese interactions. In Robert A. Kapp (Ed.), *Communicating with China* (pp. 9-27). Chicago: Intercultural Press.

O'Hair, D., Cody, M., Wang, X. T., & Chao, E. Y. (1990). Vocal stress and deception detection among Chinese. *Communication Quarterly, 38,* 158-169.

Pierson, H. D., & Bond, M. H. (1982). How do Chinese bilinguals respond to variations of interviewer language and ethnicity? *Journal of Language and Social Psychology, 1,* 123-139.

Potter, S. H. (1988). The cultural construction of emotion in rural Chinese social life. *Ethos, 16,* 181-208.

Pye, L. (1982). *Chinese commercial negotiating style.* Cambridge, MA: Oelgeschlager, Gunn & Hain.

Pye, L. (1992). *Chinese negotiating style: Commercial approaches and cultural principles.* New York: Quorum.

Redding, G. S., & Ng, M. (1982). The role of "face" in the organizational perceptions of Chinese managers. *Organization Studies, 3,* 201-219.

Schneider, M. J. (1985). Verbal and nonverbal indices of the communicative performance and acculturation of Chinese immigrants. *International Journal of Intercultural Relations, 9,* 271-283.

Scollon, R., & Scollon, S. W. (1991). Mass and count nouns in Chinese and English: A few further Whorfian considerations. In R. Blust (Ed.), *Currents in Pacific linguistics: Papers on Austronesian languages and ethnolinguistics in honor of George W. Grace* (pp. 465-475). Canberra, Australia: Pacific Linguistics.

Scollon, R., & Scollon, S. W. (1995). *Intercultural communication: A discourse approach.* Oxford, UK: Blackwell.

Smith, D. C. (1991). Children of China: An inquiry into the relationship between Chinese family life and academic achievement in modern Taiwan. *Asian Culture Quarterly, 14*(1), 1-29.

Stipek, D., Weiner, B., & Li, K. (1989). Testing some attribution-emotion relations in the People's Republic of China. *Journal of Personality and Social Psychology, 56,* 109-116.

Storti, C. (1994). *Cross-cultural dialogues.* Yarmouth, ME: Intercultural Press.

Sue, D. W., & Sue, S. (1973). Understanding Asian Americans: The neglected minority, an overview. *Personnel and Guidance Journal, 51,* 387-389.

Sun, L. K. (1991). Contemporary Chinese culture: Structure and emotionality. *Australian Journal of Chinese Affairs, 26,* 1-42.

Sun, L. J. (1994). Tan tao zhong guo ren xing ge zhi li lun xin chu fa dian [A new starting point for the inquiry about Chinese personality theories]. In Y. Bo (Ed.) *Zhong guo ren, ni shou le shen me zhu zhou?* (pp. 35-45). Taipei, Taiwan: Xing guang chu ban she.

Taylor, R. (1989). Chinese hierarchy in comparative perspectives. *Journal of Asian Studies, 48,* 490-511.

Tetlock, P. E. (1980). Explaining teacher explanations of pupil performance: A self-presentation interpretation. *Social Psychology Quarterly, 43,* 283-290.

Ting-Toomey, S. (1985). Toward a theory of conflict and culture. In W. B. Gudykunst, L. Stewart, & S. Ting-Toomey (Eds.), *Communication, culture, and organizational processes* (pp. 71-85). Beverly Hills, CA: Sage.

Ting-Toomey, S. (1988). Intercultural conflict styles: A face-negotiation theory. In Y. Y. Kim & W. B. Gudykunst (Eds.), *Theories in intercultural communication* (pp. 213-235). Newbury Park, CA: Sage.

Ting-Toomey, S., Gao, G., Trubisky, P., Yang, Z. Z., Kim, H. S., Lin, S. L., & Nishida, T. (1991). Culture, face maintenance, and styles of handling interpersonal conflict: A study in five cultures. *International Journal of Conflict Management, 2,* 275-296.

Triandis, H. (1988). Collectivism vs individualism: A reconceptualization of a basic concept in cross-cultural psychology. In C. Bagley & G. Verma (Eds.),

Cross-cultural studies of personality, attitudes, and cognition (pp. 60-95). London: Macmillan.

Triandis, H. (1995). *Individualism and collectivism.* Boulder, CO: Westview.

Tseng, W. S. (1973). The concept of personality in Confucian thought. *Psychiatry, 36,* 191-202.

Tseng, W. S., & Wu, D. Y. (Eds.). (1985). *Chinese culture and mental health.* Orlando, FL: Academic Press.

Wall, J. A., Jr., & Blum, M. (1991). Community mediation in the People's Republic of China. *Journal of Conflict Resolution, 35,* 3-20.

Wallach, J., & Metcalf, G. (1995). *Working with Americans: A practical guide for Asians on how to succeed with U.S. managers.* Singapore: McGraw-Hill.

Wang, Y. L. (1990). Ren qing sheng suo, mian zi gong fu: zhong guo ren de quan mou zhi dao [Ren qing and mian zi]. In *Zhong guo ren de xin li: Vol. 3. Zhong guo ren de mian ju xing ge: Ren qing yu mian zi* (pp. 40-52). Taipei, Taiwan: Zhang lao shi chu ban she.

Wen, C. Y. (1990). Bao de die ti liu bian [Bao and its turns/changes]. In *Zhong guo ren de xing li: Vol. 8. Zhong guo ren de shi jian you xi: Ren qing yu shi gu* (pp. 14-19). Tapei, Taiwan: Zhang lao shi chu ban she.

Wheeler, L., Reis, H. T., & Bond, M. H. (1989). Collectivism-individualism in everyday social life: The middle kingdom and the melting pot. *Journal of Personality and Social Psychology, 57,* 79-86.

White, W. G., & Chan, E. (1983). A comparison of self-concept scores of Chinese and white graduate students and professionals. *Journal of Non-White Concerns, 11,* 138-141.

Whyte, M. K. (1991). Introduction. In R. F. Dernberger, K. J. DeWoskin, J. M. Goldstein, R. Murphey, & M. K. Whyte (Eds.), *The Chinese* (pp. 295-313). Ann Arbor: University of Michigan, Center for Chinese Studies.

Wiemann, J., Chen, V., & Giles, H. (1986, November). *Beliefs about talk and silence in a cultural context.* Paper presented to the Speech Communication Association, Chicago.

Wierzbicka, A. (1996). Contrastive sociolinguistics and the theory of "cultural scripts": Chinese vs English. In M. Hellinger & U. Ammon (Eds.), *Contrastive sociolinguistics* (pp. 313-344). Berlin: de Gruyter.

Wong, G., & Stewart, S. (1990). Confucian family values: Lessons for the West. *The World & I, 5,* 523-535.

Wu, D. Y. H. (1982). Psychotherapy and emotion in traditional Chinese medicine. In A. J. Marsella & G. M. White (Eds.), *Cultural conceptions of mental health and therapy* (pp. 285-301). Dordrecht, The Netherlands: Reidel.

Wu, D. Y. H. (1996). Chinese childhood socialization. In M. H. Bond (Ed.), *The handbook of Chinese psychology* (pp. 143-154). Hong Kong: Oxford University Press.

Wu, P.-Y. (1984). Varieties of the Chinese self. In V. Kavolis (Ed.), *Designs of selfhood* (pp. 107-131). Cranbury, NJ: Associated University Presses.

Yan, J. J. (1987). Guan yu jian li zhong guo gou tong xue de gou xiang [On establishing the field of Chinese communication]. *Xing wen xue kan, 10,* 50-53.

Yang, K. S. (1981). Social orientation and individual modernity among Chinese students in Taiwan. *Journal of Social Psychology, 113,* 159-170.

Yang, K. S. (1990a). Bao de gong neng yu bian qian [Bao's functions and changes]. In *Zhong guo ren de xing li: Vol. 8. Zhong guo ren de shi jian you xi: Ren qing yu shi gu* (pp. 28-34). Tapei, Taiwan: Zhang lao shi chu ban she.

Yang, K. S. (1990b). Xian dai she hui zhong de "Ren qing" [Ren qing in modern society]. In *Zhong guo ren de xing li: Vol. 8. Zhong guo ren de shi jian you xi: Ren qing yu shi gu* (pp. 101-104). Tapei, Taiwan: Zhang lao shi chu ban she.

Yang, L. S. (1957). The concept of pao as a basis for social relations in China. In J. K. Fairbank (Ed.), *Chinese thought and institutions* (pp. 291-309). Chicago: University of Chicago Press.

Yang, M. J., & Hwang, K. K. (1980). The wedge model of self-disclosure and its correlates. *Acta Psychologica Taiwanica, 22,* 51-70.

Young, L. W. L. (1994). *Crosstalk and culture in Sino-American communication.* Cambridge, UK: Cambridge University Press.

Yu, D. H. (1990). Zhong guo ren xin di de gu shi [The hidden stories of Chinese]. In *Zhong guo ren de xin li: Vol. 3. Zhong guo ren de mian ju xing ge: Ren qing yu mian zi* (pp. 63-107). Taipei, Taiwan: Zhang lao shi chu ban she.

Yu, D. H., & Gu, B. L. (1990). Zhong guo ren de qing mian jiao lu [Chinese face concerns]. In *Zhong guo ren de xin li: Vol. 3. Zhong guo ren de mian ju xing ge: Ren qing yu mian zi* (pp. 63-107). Taipei, Taiwan: Zhang lao shi chu ban she.

Yum, J. O. (1991). The impact of Confucianism on interpersonal relationships and communication patterns in East Asia. In L. A. Samovar & R. E. Porter (Eds.), *Intercultural communication: A reader* (6th ed., pp. 185-192). Belmont, CA: Wadsworth.

Zhang, S. Y. (1994). Wo kan chou lou de zhong guo ren [Reading *The ugly Chinese*]. In Y. Bo. (Ed.), *Zhong guo ren, ni shou le shen me zhu zhou?* (pp. 95-102). Taipei, Taiwan: Xing guang chu ban she.

Zheng, X. L., (Producer), Zheng, X. L., & Feng, X. G. (Directors). (1993). *A native of Beijing in New York* [TV Series, Part IX]. Beijing, China: Chinese Central Television Station, Beijing Television and Arts Center, and Chinese Central Television Production Center.

Zhu, R. L. (1990). Biao da xing ren qing yu gong ju xing ren qing [Expressive and instrumental ren qing]. In *Zhong guo ren de xin li: Vol. 8. Zhong guo ren de shi jian you xi: Ren qing yu shi gu* (pp. 120-127). Taipei, Taiwan: Zhang lao shi chu ban she.

Zhuang, H. Q. (1990). Zhan sheng zi ji nei xin de di ren [Defeating the internal enemy]. In *Zhong guo ren de xin li: Vol. 3. Zhong guo ren de mian ju xing ge: Ren qing yu mian zi* (pp. 109-119). Taipei, Taiwan: Zhang lao shi chu ban she.

Index

103

About the Authors

Ge Gao is Associate Professor in the Department of Communication Studies at San Jose State University. Her research interests include Chinese communication processes, cross-cultural interpersonal relationship development, and intercultural communication. Her publications have appeared in the *International Journal of Intercultural Relations, Communication Quarterly,* and *Communication Research Reports,* among others.

Stella Ting-Toomey is Professor of Speech Communication at California State University, Fullerton. She is author and editor of 10 books. Three recent book titles are *The Challenge of Facework: Cross-Cultural and Interpersonal Issues; Building Bridges: Interpersonal Skills for a Changing World* (coauthor); and *Communication in Personal Relationships Across Cultures* (coeditor). She has published extensively on cross-cultural facework, intercultural conflict, Asian communication patterns, and the effective identity negotiation model. She has held major leadership roles in international communication associations and has served on numerous editorial boards. She has lectured widely throughout the United States, Asia, and Europe on the topic of intercultural facework management. She is an experienced trainer in the area of transcultural competence.